First World War
and Army of Occupation
War Diary
France, Belgium and Germany

48 DIVISION
144 Infantry Brigade,
Brigade Machine Gun Company
23 January 1915 - 24 April 1916

WO95/2759/3

The Naval & Military Press Ltd
www.nmarchive.com
Published in association with The National Archives

Published by

The Naval & Military Press Ltd

Unit 10 Ridgewood Industrial Park,

Uckfield, East Sussex,

TN22 5QE England

Tel: +44 (0) 1825 749494

www.naval-military-press.com

www.nmarchive.com

This diary has been reprinted in facsimile from the original. Any imperfections are inevitably reproduced and the quality may fall short of modern type and cartographic standards.

© **Crown Copyright**
Images reproduced by permission of The National Archives, London, England, 2015.

Contents

Document type	Place/Title	Date From	Date To
Heading	144 Machine Gun Co. Jan Vol I		
War Diary	Couin	23/01/1915	27/01/1915
War Diary		27/01/1916	31/01/1916
War Diary	Hebutherne & Couin	02/02/1916	02/02/1916
War Diary	Couin & Bus.	03/02/1916	03/02/1916
War Diary	Bus	04/02/1916	13/02/1916
War Diary	Hannescamps	13/02/1916	14/02/1916
War Diary	Bienvillers	15/02/1916	29/02/1916
Heading	War Diary of Machine Gun Company 144th Infantry Brigade. From 1st March to 31st March 1916. Volume 3.		
War Diary	Souastre	01/03/1916	11/03/1916
War Diary	Colincamps	14/03/1916	31/03/1916
Heading	War Diary of Machine Gun Company 144 Infantry Brigade from 1st April 1916 to 30th April 1916. Volume IV.		
War Diary	Colincamps	31/03/1916	02/04/1916
War Diary	Sailly	04/04/1916	26/04/1916
Heading	War Diary of Machine Gun Company 144th Infantry Brigade From 1st May 1916 to 31st May 1916 Volume 5.		
War Diary	Sailly	01/05/1916	04/05/1916
War Diary	Beauval	05/05/1916	14/05/1916
War Diary	Couins	15/05/1916	15/05/1916
War Diary	Sailly	16/05/1916	31/05/1916
Heading	War Diary Machine Gun Company 144th Infantry Brigade. From 1st June 1916 to 30th June 1916 (Volume 6)		
War Diary	Sailly Au Bois	01/06/1916	02/06/1916
War Diary	Bretel	03/06/1916	04/06/1916
War Diary	Coulinvillers	05/06/1916	14/06/1916
War Diary	Coigneux	15/06/1916	30/06/1916
War Diary	Coigneaux & Mailly-Maillet	01/07/1916	02/07/1916
War Diary	Mailly Maillet	02/07/1916	03/07/1916
War Diary	Courcelles	04/07/1916	14/07/1916
War Diary	Bouzincourt & Ovillers.	15/07/1916	17/07/1916
War Diary	Ovillers	17/07/1916	26/07/1916
War Diary	Ovillers-Buzincourt. Hedauville-Arqueves-Beauval. Franqueville	27/07/1916	30/07/1916
War Diary	Franqueville	31/07/1916	31/07/1916
Miscellaneous	Appendix 2.		
Diagram etc	Sample of Temporary M.G Emplacement Plan Section		
War Diary	Franqueville	01/08/1916	07/08/1916
War Diary	Authieux-Puchvillers Bouzincourt.	09/08/1916	13/08/1916
War Diary	Ovillers	13/08/1916	25/08/1916
War Diary	Forceville	26/08/1916	26/08/1916
War Diary	Englebelmer	27/08/1916	27/08/1916
War Diary	Mailly-Maillet	28/08/1916	31/08/1916
Heading	War Diary of 144 Machine Gun Company From 1st September 1916 to 30th September 1916 Volume 9.		

War Diary	Mailly-Maillet	01/09/1916	17/09/1916
War Diary		14/09/1916	18/09/1916
War Diary	Autheux	19/09/1916	30/09/1916
Heading	War Diary of 144 Machine Gun Company From 1st October 1916 to 31st October 1916 Volume 10.		
War Diary	Ivergny & Grenas	01/10/1916	01/10/1916
War Diary	Grenas	02/10/1916	07/10/1916
War Diary		02/10/1916	09/10/1916
War Diary	Fm Dela Breffaye	10/10/1916	14/10/1916
War Diary	Souastre	15/10/1916	17/10/1916
War Diary	Hebutherne	18/10/1916	19/10/1916
War Diary	Souastre	20/10/1916	20/10/1916
War Diary	Ivergny	21/10/1916	23/10/1916
War Diary	Ivergny & Bresle	24/10/1916	30/10/1916
War Diary	Albert	31/10/1916	01/11/1916
War Diary	Bazentin Le-Petit	02/11/1916	02/11/1916
War Diary	Martinpuich	03/11/1916	12/11/1916
War Diary	Lonely Tr. Camp.	13/11/1916	14/11/1916
War Diary	Martinpuich	15/11/1916	29/11/1916
Heading	War Diary of 144 Machine Gun Company from 1st December/16 to 31st December/16 Volume 12.		
War Diary	Shelter Wood	01/12/1916	01/12/1916
War Diary	Martin Puich	02/12/1916	04/12/1916
War Diary	Shelter Wood	06/12/1916	08/12/1916
War Diary	Martinpuich	10/12/1916	15/12/1916
War Diary	Albert	16/12/1916	31/12/1916
Heading	War Diary of 144th Machine Gun Coy. From 1st to 31st January 1917. Vol 13.		
War Diary	Vadencourt	01/01/1917	07/01/1917
War Diary		05/01/1917	05/01/1917
War Diary	Limeux	08/01/1917	27/01/1917
War Diary		10/01/1917	17/01/1917
War Diary	Limeux	25/01/1917	28/01/1917
War Diary	Cerisy.	29/01/1917	31/01/1917
Heading	War Diary of 144 Machine Gun Company from 1st February 1917 to 28th February 1917. Volume 14.		
War Diary		01/02/1917	02/02/1917
War Diary	Peronnene 62c N.W. 4.	02/02/1917	02/02/1917
War Diary	Barleoux 62c S.W. 2.	02/02/1917	02/02/1917
War Diary		03/02/1917	28/02/1917
Heading	War Diary of 144 Machine Gun Company from 1st March 1917 to 31st March 1917 Volume 15.		
War Diary	Camp 56 Cappy	01/03/1917	17/03/1917
War Diary	La Maisonnette Trenches	17/03/1917	20/03/1917
War Diary	Cappy	21/03/1917	24/03/1917
War Diary	Peronne	28/03/1917	28/03/1917
War Diary	Tincourt	29/03/1917	31/03/1917
Heading	War Diary of 144 Machine Gun Company. from 1st April 1917 to 30th April 1917. Volume 16.		
War Diary	Longavesnes	01/04/1917	02/04/1917
War Diary	Tincourt Wood	02/04/1917	06/04/1917
War Diary	Villers Faucon	07/04/1917	13/04/1917
War Diary	Tincourt Wood	14/04/1917	19/04/1917
War Diary	Villers Faucon	20/04/1917	30/04/1917
Diagram etc	Rough Sketch Map Showing Units of advance during open war from between 29th March & 8th April 1917.		

War Diary	Appendix 13.	24/04/1917	24/04/1917
Miscellaneous	Statement of Casualties for month ending 30th April 1917.	30/04/1917	30/04/1917
Heading	War Diary of 144th Machine Gun Company 1st May to 31st May 1917 (Vol. XVII).		
War Diary	Templeux	01/05/1917	01/05/1917
War Diary	Villers Faucon	02/05/1917	02/05/1917
War Diary	Tincourt	04/05/1917	05/05/1917
War Diary	Buire	06/05/1917	11/05/1917
War Diary	Peronne	12/05/1917	12/05/1917
War Diary	Combles	13/05/1917	13/05/1917
War Diary	Fremicourt	14/05/1917	18/05/1917
War Diary	Morchies	21/05/1917	28/05/1917
War Diary		27/05/1917	30/05/1917
Miscellaneous	Statement of Casualties for month ending 31.5.17.		
Heading	144 Machine Gun Company War Diary from 1st June 1917 to 30th June 1917. Volume 18.		
Heading	War Diary of 144th Machine Gun Company 1st June to 30th June 1917 (Vol XVIII).		
War Diary	Haplincourt	01/06/1917	05/06/1917
War Diary	Morchies	06/06/1917	15/06/1917
War Diary	Haplincourt	16/06/1917	30/06/1917
Miscellaneous	144 Machine Gun Company. Statement of Casualties etc June 1917.		
Heading	War Diary of 144 Machine Gun Company from 1st July 1917 to 31st July 1917. Volume 19.		
War Diary	Haplincourt	01/07/1917	01/07/1917
War Diary	Achiet-Le-Petit	02/07/1917	03/07/1917
War Diary	Blairville	04/07/1917	09/07/1917
War Diary	St. Omer	10/07/1917	21/07/1917
War Diary	A.29.c.32.52. (Map Belgium Sheet 28 N.W. 1/20000)	22/07/1917	26/07/1917
War Diary	A.29.c.32.52.	27/07/1917	31/07/1917
Miscellaneous	Appendix A.		
Miscellaneous	Statement of Casualties etc. July 1917.		
Heading	War Diary of 144 M.G. Coy from 1st August 1917 to 31st August 1917. Volume 20.		
War Diary	A.3.q.32.52.	01/08/1917	05/08/1917
War Diary	Dambre Camp	06/08/1917	31/08/1917
Miscellaneous	Statement of Casualties August, 1917.		
Heading	War Diary of 144 Machine Gun Company from 1st September 1917 to 30th September 1917. Volume 21		
War Diary	School Camp	01/09/1917	01/09/1917
War Diary	Jan-Ter-Biezen	01/09/1917	18/09/1917
War Diary	Bertehem	19/09/1917	30/09/1917
Miscellaneous	Statement of Casualties etc.		
Heading	War Diary of 144 Machine Gun Company from 1st October 1917 to 31st October 1917. Volume 22.		
War Diary	Berteham	01/10/1917	01/10/1917
War Diary	Brake Camp	02/10/1917	03/10/1917
War Diary	Line & Reigersburg	04/10/1917	04/10/1917
War Diary	Reigersburg Camp	05/10/1917	08/10/1917
War Diary	Line	09/10/1917	10/10/1917
War Diary	Siege Camp	11/10/1917	11/10/1917
War Diary	School Camp	12/10/1917	13/10/1917
War Diary	Savy	14/10/1917	14/10/1917
War Diary	Villers-Au-Bois	15/10/1917	15/10/1917

War Diary	Line	16/10/1917	16/10/1917
War Diary	Chaudiere Sector	16/10/1917	31/10/1917
Miscellaneous	Statement of Casualties October 1917		
Map	Chaudiere Sector		
Miscellaneous	Dispositions	01/11/1917	01/11/1917
Miscellaneous	Dispositions	16/10/1917	16/10/1917
Map	Chaudiere Sector		
Heading	War Diary of 1/8th Bn Worcestershire Regt. Feby. 1st to Feby 28th 1917 (Vol XXIII)		
War Diary	Bienviller	29/02/1916	29/02/1916
Heading	144th Brigade. 48th Division. 1/7th Battalion Worcestershire Regiment February 1916.		
Heading	144th Brigade. 48th Division. 1/7th Battalion Worcestershire Regiment March 1916.		
Heading	144th Brigade. 48th Division. 1/7th Battalion Worcestershire Regiment April 1916.		
Heading	144th Brigade. 48th Division. 1/7th Battalion Worcestershire Regiment May 1916.		
Heading	144th Brigade. 48th Division. 1/7th Battalion Worcestershire Regiment June 1916. Appendices attached:- Schemes for raids.		
Miscellaneous	Raid of German Trenches night 15th/16th June 1916 by 7th Battalion The Worcestershire Regiment.	16/06/1916	16/06/1916
Miscellaneous	Scheme for Raid by 7th Battalion the Worcestershire Regiment, Night 28/29th June, 1916.	29/06/1916	29/06/1916
Heading	144th Inf. Bde. 48th Div. War Diary 1/7th Battn. The Worcestershire Regiment. July 1916.		
Heading	144th Brigade. 48th Division. 1/7th Battalion Worcestershire Regiment August 1916.		
Heading	144th Brigade. 48th Division. 1/7th Battalion Worcestershire Regiment September 1916.		
Heading	144th Brigade. 48th Division. 1/7th Battalion Worcestershire Regiment October 1916.		
Heading	144th Brigade. 48th Division. 1/7th Battalion Worcestershire Regiment November 1916.		
Heading	144th Brigade. 48th Division. 1/7th Battalion Worcestershire Regiment December 1916.		
Miscellaneous	Report on Fighting Patrol sent out by 1/7th Bn. The Worcestershire Regt., near The Butte De Warlencourt. App B.	04/12/1916	04/12/1916
Map	Scale-1/20,000.		
Map	Part of 62c N.E.		
Miscellaneous	Operations Against Epehy 30-31 March, 1.2.3 April 1917.	30/03/1917	30/03/1917
Miscellaneous			
Miscellaneous	Operations of the 1/7th. Battalion The Worcestershire Regiment 16th.-17th. August 1917.	16/08/1917	16/08/1917
Miscellaneous			
Miscellaneous	Report on Operations of The 1/7th. Battalion The Worcestershire Regt. 8th.-9th.-10th. October 1917	09/10/1917	09/10/1917
Miscellaneous	Answers to questions by G.O.C. Division on Operations 9th.-10th-11th. October 1917.	09/10/1917	11/10/1917
Heading	48th Division 144th Infy Bde 1-8th Bn Worcs Regt Apr 1915-1917 Oct. To Italy.		

Heading	144th Inf. Bde. 48th Div. Battn. Disembarked Boulogne from England 1.4.15 1/8th Battn. The Worcestershire Regiment. April 1915-Aug 1918.		
Heading	144th Inf. Bde. 48th Div. 1/8th Battn. The Worcestershire Regiment. May (5.5.15-31.5.15) 1915.		
Heading	144th Inf. Bde. 48th Div. 1/8th Battn. The Worcestershire Regiment. June (4.6.15 to 29.6.15) 1915.		
Heading	144th Inf. Bde. 48th Div. 1/8th Battn. The Worcestershire Regiment. July 1915.		
Heading	144th Inf. Bde. 48th Div. 1/8th Battn. The Worcestershire Regiment. August 1915.		
Heading	144th Inf. Bde. 48th Div. 1/8th Battn. The Worcestershire Regiment. September 1915.		
Heading	144th Inf. Bde. 48th Div. 1/8th Battn. The Worcestershire Regiment. October 1915.		
Heading	144th Inf. Bde. 48th Div. 1/8th Battn. The Worcestershire Regiment. November 1915.		
Heading	144th Inf. Bde. 48th Div. 1/8th Battn. The Worcestershire Regiment. December 1915.		
Heading	144th Brigade. 48th Division. 1/8th Battalion Worcestershire Regiment January 1916.		
Heading	144th Brigade. 48th Division. 1/8th Battalion Worcestershire Regiment. February 1916.		
Heading	144th Brigade. 48th Division. 1/8th Battalion Worcestershire Regiment March 1916.		
Heading	144th Brigade. 48th Division. 1/8th Battalion Worcestershire Regiment April 1916.		
Heading	144th Brigade. 48th Division. 1/8th Battalion Worcestershire Regiment. May 1916.		
Heading	144th Brigade. 48th Division. 1/8th Battalion Worcestershire Regiment. June 1916.		
Heading	144th Inf. Bde. 48th Div. War Diary 1/8th Battn. The Worcestershire Regiment. July 1916.		
Heading	144th Brigade 48th Division 1/8th Battalion Worcestershire Regiment August 1916.		
Heading	144th Brigade. 48th Division. 1/8th Battalion Worcestershire Regiment. September 1916.		
Heading	144th Brigade. 48th Division. 1/8th Battalion Worcestershire Regiment October 1916.		
Heading	144th Brigade. 48th Division. 1/8th Battalion Worcestershire Regiment November 1916.		
Heading	144th Brigade. 48th Division. 1/8th Battalion Worcestershire Regiment December 1916.		
Miscellaneous			
Miscellaneous	Operations of the 9th October 1917. Appendix A.	09/10/1917	09/10/1917
Operation(al) Order(s)	1/8th Bn The Worcestershire Regt. Operation Order No. 10. Appendix B.	17/10/1917	17/10/1917
Operation(al) Order(s)	1/8th Bn The Worcestershire Regt. Operation Order No. 11. Appendix C.	21/10/1917	21/10/1917
Operation(al) Order(s)	1/8th Bn The Worcestershire Regt. Operation Order No. 12. Appendix D.	25/10/1917	25/10/1917
Operation(al) Order(s)	1/8th Bn The Worcestershire Regt. Operation Order No. 13. Appendix E.	29/10/1917	29/10/1917
Heading	48th Division 144th Infy Bde 144th Machine Gun Coy Jan 1916-1917 Oct. To Italy.		

Heading	144th Brigade. 48th Division. 144th Brigade Machine Gun Company January 1916-Feb 1918.		
Heading	144th Brigade. 48th Division. 144th Brigade Machine Gun Company February 1916.		
Heading	War Diary of Machine Gun Company 144th Infantry Brigade from 1st February 1916 to 29th February 1916 (Volume 2)		
Heading	144th Brigade. 48th Division. 144th Brigade Machine Gun Company March 1916.		
Heading	144th Brigade 48th Division. 144th Brigade Machine Gun Company April 1916.		
Heading	144th Brigade. 48th Division. 144th Brigade Machine Gun Company May 1916.		
Heading	144th Brigade. 48th Division. 144th Brigade Machine Gun Company June 1916.		
Heading	144th Inf. Bde. 48th Div. War Diary 144th Machine Gun Company. July 1916.		
Heading	Appendices I II III		
War Diary	Ovillers	16/07/1916	17/07/1916
War Diary	Ovillers	22/07/1916	23/07/1916
Heading	144th Brigade 48th Division. 144th Brigade Machine Gun Company August 1916.		
Heading	144th Brigade. 48th Division. 144th Brigade Machine Gun Company September 1916.		
Heading	144th Brigade. 48th Division. 144th Brigade Machine Gun Company October 1916.		
Heading	144th Brigade. 48th Division. 144th Brigade Machine Gun Company November 1916.		
Heading	144th Brigade. 48th Division. 144th Brigade Machine Gun Company December 1916.		
Miscellaneous	Operation during period 1st April to 13th April 1917. Appendix A.	01/04/1917	01/04/1917
Miscellaneous	144. Machine Gun Company. List of Casualties for the month of August 1917.		
Miscellaneous	144. Machine Gun Company. Report on operations:- 4th. October, and 9th. & 10th. October, 1917.	04/10/1917	04/10/1917
Miscellaneous	144 Machine Gun Company. Report on operations 9th. and 10th. October 1917.	09/10/1917	09/10/1917
War Diary		20/02/1916	28/02/1916
War Diary	Courcelles	20/03/1916	23/03/1916
War Diary	Trenches 57D. K.34	24/03/1916	27/03/1916
War Diary	Colincamps 57.N K.25C	28/03/1916	31/03/1916
War Diary		01/05/1916	01/05/1916
War Diary	Couin	02/05/1916	03/05/1916
War Diary	Beauval	04/05/1916	08/05/1916
War Diary		31/05/1916	31/05/1916
War Diary	W.8.d.	14/08/1916	16/08/1916
War Diary	V.12.c.	17/08/1916	18/08/1916
War Diary	X.3.c.6.8	19/08/1916	20/08/1916
War Diary	X.8.a.8.5	20/08/1916	21/08/1916
War Diary	X.2.a.8.5.	22/08/1916	23/08/1916
War Diary	V.12.c.	24/08/1916	26/08/1916
War Diary	Forceville	27/08/1916	27/08/1916
War Diary	Q.9.b.9.3.	28/08/1916	31/08/1916
War Diary	Huppy	08/01/1917	26/01/1917
War Diary	Cappy	09/03/1917	13/03/1917

War Diary	Support Trenches	14/03/1917	16/03/1917
War Diary	Le Mesnil	21/03/1917	21/03/1917
War Diary	Achille Ravine	22/03/1917	25/03/1917
War Diary	Poperinghe	27/07/1917	31/07/1917
War Diary		05/03/1916	06/03/1916
War Diary	Colincamps.	07/03/1916	07/03/1916
War Diary	Trenches Opposite Serre	11/03/1916	12/03/1916
War Diary	Bouzincourt	19/07/1916	20/07/1916
Heading	WO95/2759-3 144 Bde MG Coy Jan 1916-Oct 1917.		
War Diary	Sailly	27/04/1916	27/04/1916
War Diary	Martinpuich	15/04/1916	24/04/1916
Diagram etc			
Heading	War Diary of 144 Machine Gun Company from 1st November 1916 to 30th November 1916. Volume XI.		

144 machine gun Co.

Jan 1 1904

45

WAR DIARY or INTELLIGENCE SUMMARY.

Army Form C. 2118.

Machine Gun Company
144th Infantry Brigade
~~10th Battn. The Worcester Regt~~

Place	Date	Hour	Summary of Events and Information	Remarks and references to Appendices
COULIN	1915 Jan 23rd		The Company mobilized at COULIN at 10am and was billetted in huts at CHATEAU PARK. Personnel was drawn from Units in the 144th Infantry Brigade as follows :—	
			4th Gloucester Regt 2 Officers + 33 other ranks, 2 M.G. limbers + 8 draught.	
			6th Gloucester Regt 2 Officers + 35 " " " " " "	
			7th Worcester Regt 2 Officers + 34 " " " " " "	
			8th Worcester Regt 1 Officer + 35 " " " " " "	
			8th Essex Regt 1 Officer attached to 8th Worcester Regt.	
			48th Divisional Train 1 Water cart + 2 draught, 1 Cook's cart + draught, 4 Limber waggons	
			G.S. for S.A.A. + 8 draught.	
			144th Infantry Brigade 1 Officer seconded from 8th Bn. Worcester Regt + 2 other ranks attached from 8th Bn. Worcester Regt. + 1 Officer's charger	
			N.B. At this time 1 officer + 2 other ranks were in hospital.	2 men joined from R.A.M.C. LOUVENCOURT
	24th		Working parties worked on Company Stables + hutments. Aircraft gun fired on enemy plane.	
	25th		Working parties supervised by "Air Craft" + 2 other guns fired on Nest of enemy planes.	
	26th		Preparation for trenches.	
	27th		Relieved Machine Gun Company 145th Infantry Brigade in Sector of trenches EAST of	

WAR DIARY
of
INTELLIGENCE SUMMARY.
(Erase heading not required.)

Army Form C. 2118.

Machine Gun Company
144 n. Infantry Brigade

Place	Date	Hour	Summary of Events and Information	Remarks and references to Appendices
	1916 Jan 27th		HEBUTHERNE Dispositions as follows:— 4 Guns in G Section, 2 Guns behind G Section — 2 Guns in H Section & 2 Guns in reserve behind J Section — 2 Guns in K Section — 4 Guns in HEBUTHERNE KEEP — rifle battery in H, J & K Section	
	28th		Very Quiet — Work. Emplacement started in TRENCH WAGRAM — Renovation of KEEP Emplacements Clearing of Trenches near Emplacements in G Section — Work on Company Head Quarters	
	29th 30th		Work as before — Cooperated with infantry artillery in assisting infantry in raids on Enemy Trenches during early morning of 30th inst. One of our patrols particularly on Value of assistance given by machine gun fire — One casualty	
	31st		Work as usual.	
			N.B. During this period it has been found that after deducting transport and other necessary details the number of N.C.O's + men available for duty with the Guns Guns on an average 1 N.C.O & 3 or 4 Gun numbers on each Gun. During this personnel double sentries by night & single sentries by day have to be found in addition to men for ordinary work. Section & Gun duties will reduce even these numbers & sustained action even with all Guns would be impossible owing to shortage of personnel. Transport. In order that the Transport Sergeant should Carry out his duties efficiently he should be mounted & this is not allowed for on The Establishment. Given that the Company is on Motive the Transport 5 mules back & Batman Gun. + Therefore act as Grooms as well as servants.	

1577   Wt. W10791/1773   500,000   1/15   D.D. & L.   A.D.S.S./Forms/C. 2118.

Army Form C. 2118.

WAR DIARY or INTELLIGENCE SUMMARY.
(Erase heading not required.)

Machine Gun Company
144th Infantry Brigade

Instructions regarding War Diaries and Intelligence Summaries are contained in F. S. Regs., Part II. and the Staff Manual respectively. Title pages will be prepared in manuscript.

Place	Date	Hour	Summary of Events and Information	Remarks and references to Appendices
	1916 Feb			
HEBUTERNE & COLLIN	2		Relieved by M.G. Coy 145th Infantry Brigade & returned to hutments at Collin. During the tour in the trenches the Company had 1 casualty (accidental G.S.W. in right hand)	
COLLIN & BUS	3		Company left Collin at 10am & marched to Bus taking up billets in CHATEAU PARK.	
BUS	4		Cleaning of Guns & Equipment.	
"	5		Daily classes in mechanism & immediate action	
"			All guns were Strit & Armoury at AUTHIE & overhauled.	
"	11			
"	6		Pte. Moses dispatched to Base. Time expired	
"	11		Sgt Barclay dispatched to Transport Course — Pte Baumer dispatched to Base Time Expired	
"	12		Pte Preparation for Trenches Lt. Thomas, Corp Tombs, Pte Melvin, Pte Steele dispatched to M.G. Course G.H.Q.	
"	13		Relieved Machine Gun Section 112 K Inf Brigade in trenches N. of FONQUEVILLERS [Nos SC-76 E.28.a.88 – E.11.a.67]	NEW EDITION FONQUEVILLERS 57D HQ MAPS 57
			Company left Bus at 12.30pm. Dispositions as follows:—	
			A One section in Brigade reserve BIENVILLERS. One section in HANNESCAMPS. One Section in trenches BIENVILLERS F.10.c.40.65. These guns will replace the defence to be referred to as F.D. Nos 3 - 6	
			E.10.D.00.25 – E.10.C.50.20 – F.10.C.40.40.	
			Gun Section (H.Q. FONQUEVILLERS) with two guns (Village defence) F.D. 1 & 2 at E.21.D.90.50 & E.21.B.60.40	

T/134. Wt. W708–776. 500000. 4/15. Sir J. C. & B.

Army Form C. 2118.

Warwick Gun Company

INTELLIGENCE SUMMARY.
(Erase heading not required.)

Machine Gun Company
14th Inf. Brigade

Instructions regarding War Diaries and Intelligence Summaries are contained in F. S. Regs., Part II. and the Staff Manual respectively. Title pages will be prepared in manuscript.

Place	Date	Hour	Summary of Events and Information	Remarks and references to Appendices
HANNESCAMPS	1916 Feb 13.		* Two Guns in or front behind front line Trenches. No1 Gun E22 B20.50. No2 Gun E22 B10.70. One Section with Reserve in or front behind front line. No3 Gun E16.D90,90. No4 Gun E17.A15,45. No5 Gun E11.B10,40. No6 Gun E11.A.80,80. Hd.qrs of the Company took over H.Q. of 11th R. WARWICK Regt in HANNESCAMPS E16.A.30,30. Transport parked in SOMASTRE	
	14th		One Casualty. S.S.W right buttock. Slight. No 2059 Pte Newman. JA — Divisional Salvage Co. 24.2.16	
BIENVILLERS	15th		Hd.quarters moved to BIENVILLERS — taking over from 8. WORCESTER REGT. [Pte WHITE reported to Base Transport] 143 Inf. Brigade took over Trenches 50 — 53 & the Village & Village defence of FONQUEVILLERS	
	16th		Heavy rain causing V.D. 3 to be untenable & all Trenches & positions almost unformable. V.D. 2 relieved by 143 Inf Brigade, & Taken R & a portion near V.D. 1. During this period it has become more than ever apparent that the personnel is totally insufficient & the least sickness or casualties will necessitate at least 1 gun being withdrawn. Weather conditions & the state of the Trenches & the amount of work & sentry duty done by all ranks is second to none on the efficiency of the Unit.	
	17th		Relief of B Section by A Section & C Section by D Section completed by 9 p.m. No 1276 Pte Wade despatched to Base (time Spine) — No 1714 Pte Knight to Div: Salvage Coy.	
	18th		About 2.30 a.m. heavy bombardment of Trs. 52 – 57. During this bombardment the two Sentries on	

T2131. Wt. W708—776. 500000. 4/15. Sir J. C. & E.

Army Form C. 2118.

Machine Gun Company
144th Infantry Brigade

INTELLIGENCE SUMMARY.
(Erase heading not required.)

Instructions regarding War Diaries and Intelligence Summaries are contained in F.S. Regs., Part II. and the Staff Manual respectively. Title pages will be prepared in manuscript.

Place	Date	Hour	Summary of Events and Information	Remarks and references to Appendices
BIENVILLERS	1916 Feb 18		No 2 Gun were knocked out – Ammunition box's broken, but Gun unimpaired. No 2537 Pte Adams Killed. No 161 Pte Faulkner wounded C.C.S. No 2 V.D. withdrawn from Sniper's Square & No 3 Gun team into reserve in HANNESCAMPS. Altered dispositions :- No 1. E.22.B.20.30 – No 2. E.22.B.10.70, No 3. E.17.A.15.45. No 4. E.11.B.10.40. No 5. E.11.A.80.80, No 7 V.D. [Sniper Square] E.21.D.90.50 – No 2 V.D. E.16.D.10.80, No 3 x D. E.10.D.00.25 – No 4 V.D. E.10.C.50.50 No 5 V.D. E.10.C.40.65 2 guns (heavy) HANNESCAMPS. 4 guns (Lewis) BIENVILLERS	
	21st		Relief of D Section by C Section & A Section by B Section Completed by 11 p.m. Very sharp frost & snow. No 1.72 Sgt Cooper dispatched to Base time expired No 2098 Pte Brown C.C.S.	Difficulty experienced with guns owing to oil freezing
	23rd 24		"	
	25		Relief of C by D & B by A Completed by 10.30 p.m. No 1886 Pte Wale M.G.S. (artificer) expired. No fork.	
	26		New positions at E.16.C.05.35 & E.16.C.95.40 started. No 1600 L. Cpl Toogood dispatched to Base time expired	
	29	3 p.m.	Relief by 112 Inf Brigade starting at 5 p.m. Company has orders to move to SOUASTRE after relief. During this period greater difficulty than ever has been experienced owing	

Confidential

War Diary

of

Machine Gun Company

144th Infantry Brigade.

from 1st March to 31st March 1916.

Volume 3.

Army Form C. 2118.

WAR DIARY
or
INTELLIGENCE SUMMARY.
(Erase heading not required.)

Machine Gun Company.
144th Infantry Brigade

Place	Date	Hour	Summary of Events and Information	Remarks and references to Appendices
SOUASTRE	1916 March 1		Reinforcement of N.C.O. & 5 men reported from M.G. Corps via STAPLES – This reinforcement chiefly of this reinforcement was poor – most of the men had only done 3 weeks on the Gun & knew nothing about a maxim – Their physique was also poor.	
	2		Preparation for trenches. Transport moved to BUS.	
	3		Relieved 13. M.G. Coy. 121st Brigade in trenches EAST of COLINCAMPS – Dispositions as follows. 8 guns in reserve in COLINCAMPS – 8 guns in action. Each section in the line had Two guns in 2nd or support line & 2 guns in Brig. Reserve line. Front line Gun No.1 Gun K.34 B.35,45. No.2 Gun K.29 C.34,45. No.3 Gun K.29 A.05,10. No.4 Gun K.33 B.55,70 (No.5) K.33 B.60,25 (No.7) K.33 B.55,70 (No.9) K.27 B.99.05 (No.10) K.27 B.60,85. Relief completed by 10.30pm. L.Cpl. Bond (reinforcement) deserted at the mouth of the new dugout	57 D N E 3rd points 57 2nd section Snow & very bad weather
	4		N.C.O. & 2 men left for M/g course at WISQUES – Lewis party (1 officer & 2 O.R.) returned.	
	6		Emplacement and dugout in TROISANCHS [Troissans] started – also trench mounting put in No.3 position	
			Battalions attached 2 men per Gun to learn m.actions.	
	8		Relief of B Section by A Section & C Section by D Section completed by 7.30pm.	
	9		Position & Emplacement started for No.7 Gun	
	10		Anti-aircraft positions started near No. 6,7,9 &10 Guns – Also 3 new COLINCAMPS	
	11		Guns sent to Armoury for overhaul. 1 new K.J.A.	

Army Form C. 2118.

WAR DIARY
or
INTELLIGENCE SUMMARY.
(Erase heading not required.)

Machine Gun Company,
144th Infantry Brigade.

Instructions regarding War Diaries and Intelligence Summaries are contained in F. S. Regs., Part II. and the Staff Manual respectively. Title pages will be prepared in manuscript.

Place	Date	Hour	Summary of Events and Information	Remarks and references to Appendices
G. IN CAMP S.	1916 March 14		Relief of A Section by B Section & D Section by C Section by 7.30 pm. Gun fault & Armoury for overhaul.	
	16		Guns in right section replied throughout the night to enemy M/guns which had caused a lot of inconvenience & some casualties to working parties & reliefs of right Battalion. Enemy M/guns eventually became much less active.	
	17		Alarm posts taken up by 2 sections in G. IN CAMP S:— 2 guns to bastions near SUCRIE K33 c 50.50 2 guns to ELLIS SQUARE K33 B 50.10 1 Gun & R Section No 8 K28 c 61.85, Moranmumum, No 15 A K27 B 61.85, BASIN WOOD K 28 C 41.30.	Gun sent to Armoury for overhaul.
	18/19		Heavy bombardment of left & left of left Battalion. Gas & Smoke shells were used & under cover of this enemy party entered line in 93.— No 3 Gun fired 3000 rounds on right line— Gun sent to reserve position on left, but very shortly withdrawn. Sgt Mullins R.F.A.	
	19		No 1319 Cpl Harrison dispatched to Base Time expired.	
	20.		No 1744 Pte. Knight & No 2019 Pte Newman returned to duty with Unit from Divisional Salvage Cy. Relief of B Sect. by A Sect. & C Sect. by D Section completed by 6.30 pm. Gun sent to Armoury for overhaul. 1 man & F.A.	
	21.		2 O.R's Ready 1 officer & 2 O.R. left G IN CAMP P.S. N. co & 2 man returned from M/gun Course.	
	23		Gun sent to Armoury for overhaul.	

Army Form C. 2118.

WAR DIARY
or
INTELLIGENCE SUMMARY.
(Erase heading not required.)

Machine Gun Company,
144th Infantry Brigade.

Place	Date	Hour	Summary of Events and Information	Remarks and references to Appendices
QUINCATIPS	1916 March 26		Relief of D Section by C Section & A Section by B Section completed by 6 p.m. B Section went into trenches with 4 N.C.O's & 13 O.R.	
	28		2 N.C.O's & 3 men reported from O.C. Machine Gun Corps Base Depot AFTER CAMIERS. This draft has a good deal better than the previous one — though 3 & 4 weeks training on No. 1533's Lap gun & No. 15535's Lap gun which amounts to much at our depot. VICKERS gun only deemed to be the average. Transport moved from Bus to COURCELLES. Gun sent to Armoury for overhaul.	
	29		2 Officers attended Divisional Gas School for instruction in use of Tubes Self Threw K.T.A. No 319 Lieut Johnson (B Section) departched to Base thus expired.	
	30		Gun sent to Armoury for overhaul.	
	31		Transport moved from COURCELLES to B COURM. During this period the usual difficulty was experienced owing to shortage in personnel both of Transport & Gun teams & if it had not been for attachment of men from battalions Guns could not possibly have been kept in action, & no work could have been done. Also this that is still armed with Maxim Guns a fact which causes all drafts to be virtually untrained on arrival.	

48

Confidential

War Diary

of

Machine Gun Company

144 Infantry Brigade

from 1st April 1916 to 30th April 1916

Volume ~~XXIV~~ IV

Army Form C. 2118.

WAR DIARY
or
INTELLIGENCE SUMMARY.
(Erase heading not required.)

Machine Gun Company,
144th Infantry Brigade.

Instructions regarding War Diaries and Intelligence Summaries are contained in F. S. Regs., Part II. and the Staff Manual respectively. Title pages will be prepared in manuscript.

Place	Date	Hour	Summary of Events and Information	Remarks and references to Appendices
COLINCAMPS	1916 March 31		During Afternoon 12-2pm heavy shell fire into the village. Considerable damage was done to billets — several ammunition boxes the splintered & a little knocked in back casing of one gun (Repair out fit used though very roughly) No casg. Pte Cartwright – wounded – C of 3 — 3 men Section Mess.	
	April 1		Gun Lead & Armoury for overhaul — Relief by 9th Inf Bde r Section to into G Section later by 1st Inf Bde announced.	
	2		A Section relieve B Section in positions A14 & No10 & took over from 1st MGr M/G Coy. (interrupted 4.65).	
			FORT BRIGGS H22D 35/60 – Fort Hawrfang to TROSSACHS (interrupted)	
			D Section relieve 1st Inf Bde M/G Coy in positions as follows —	
			2 Guns in dunes at R31 C30,20 with cleaven positions H21 D 10,15, r R21 D45, 65.	
			Also LAFAYETTE A22 B 35,20 r VERCINGETORIX A22 A 15, 55.	
	4		D Section relieved by 9th Inf Bde in positions No.s 1,2, 6 r 7.	
			B Section (2 guns) relieved by 9th Inf Bde in position No.s 3 r 9.	
			Headquarters A Section relieved in No 16 position by 9th Inf Bde.	
			New Company Dispositions	
SAILLY			TOUVENT FARM A23 C45,20 FORT BRIGGS A22 D35/60 TRENCHES A22 D35,15	

T2134. Wt. W708—776. 500000. 4/15. Sir J. C. & S.

Army Form C. 2118.

WAR DIARY
or
INTELLIGENCE SUMMARY.

Machine Gun Company,
144th Infantry Brigade.

(Erase heading not required.)

Instructions regarding War Diaries and Intelligence Summaries are contained in F. S. Regs., Part II. and the Staff Manual respectively. Title pages will be prepared in manuscript.

Place	Date	Hour	Summary of Events and Information	Remarks and references to Appendices
SAILLY	1916 April 4		LAFAYETTE H22.B55.20, VERCINGETORIX K22.A.75.55 & 3 Guns in Reserve K21.C.50.20.	
			Coy H.Q. moved to SAILLY.	
	5		2 Offices Sent fwd to Divisional Gun School.	
	7		No 1325 Sgt Griffiths dispatched to Base (time expired) Nothing Sgt Mulling from F.A. No	
			One gun moved from reserve K21.C.50.20 to position in FOURNIER. K23.C.20.90	
	9		No 1622 Sgt Stevens Dispatched to Base (time expired)	
	10		No 1528 Pte Lewis dispatched to Base (time expired) - No 2474 Pte Judge - No 2277 Pte Smith R. to F.A.	
			Relief of A Section by B Section & D Section by C Section completed by 5.30 p.m.	
	11		No 2277 Pte Smith R to C.C.S. - Gun sent to Armoury for new barrel	
			No 1704 Pte Clark J. to F.A. - Draw back 7off = 2 O.R.	
			No 885 Pte Weale to F.A. No 2544. Pte Badger from F.A.	
	12		Gun sent to Armoury for new barrel.	
	13		No 1795 Pte Clark G. to F.A.	
	14		No 1761 Pte Hotchings to F.A.	
	16		No 2096 Pte Martin to F.A.	
	17		No 7276 Pte Shelton M.G.C. taken on strength. Gun moved from K21.C.50.20 to position MARIE LOUISE H22.B55.30.	

Army Form C. 2118.

WAR DIARY
or
INTELLIGENCE SUMMARY.

**Machine Gun Company,
144th Infantry Brigade.**

(Erase heading not required.)

Instructions regarding War Diaries and Intelligence Summaries are contained in F. S. Regs., Part II. and the Staff Manual respectively. Title pages will be prepared in manuscript.

Place	Date	Hour	Summary of Events and Information	Remarks and references to Appendices
SAILLY	1916 April			
	18		Leave party returned. Noisex & Davis A.P.A. — A Section relieves B Section & D Section relieves C Section. 1 Cpt	
	19		Relief complete by 3 p.m.	
	20		No. 15282 2nd Cpl. Davis K.C.B. Gun hurt to Armoury for repair. 9/32 Inf Brigade relieves A Section in following position :- Touvent Farm — Trossacres — D Section relieves A Section in Fournier. A Section came back to reserve. Drafts 5 men M.G.C. taken on strength M.G	
	21		D Section relieved by 145 Inf Bde M.G.Coy at fortification :-	
	22 / 24		Training	
	25.		A & B Sections relieved 145 Inf Bde M.G.Co in trenches East of Hebuterne (Sectors Q, T, R.) 4th Bn with following dispositions:- Auran, Lafayette, Fort Briggs, Vercingetorix, Wagram. K11 d.4.9.15 Square K6.B 10.80 Pelissier K18 A90.50 Lot Mill K8 D 90.80 Maria Louise	
			Guns moved from K11 D 10.40 to Tournier. Leave party (3 OR) left.	
	26		B & C Sections relieved MS M.G 3 Inf Bde M.Gun Coy in trenches East of Fonquevillers (Section L & M) with dispositions as follows :- K3 D.1.9 — K3 B2.5, E29 A 8.6, E29 A 5.3, E26 B 9.1, E27 A 8.3 E27 B 6.3, E21 D 9.1.	

48

Vol 5

Confidential

War Diary
of
Machine Gun Company
144th Infantry Brigade
from 1st May 1916 to 31st May 1916.

Volume 5

Army Form C. 2118.

Machine Gun Company,
144th Infantry Brigade.

WAR DIARY
or
INTELLIGENCE SUMMARY.
(Erase heading not required.)

Instructions regarding War Diaries and Intelligence Summaries are contained in F.S. Regs., Part II. and the Staff Manual respectively. Title pages will be prepared in manuscript.

Place	Date	Hour	Summary of Events and Information	Remarks and references to Appendices
SAILLY	1916 May 1		B & E Sections relieved in trenches EAST of FONQUEVILLERS by 143 Inf Bde M/G Coy. Returned to billets in SAILLY	
	2		A & D Sections relieved in trenches East of HEBUTERNE by 145 Inf Bde M.G. Coy — N⁰11143 Corp. Parsons dispatched to Base time expired. (Leave possibly expires.)	1 off 2 OR. 1 off 2 OR
	3		Drew VICKERS Guns and Tripods MAXIMS. and Spare Parts — N⁰1649 Sgt Mullings — N⁰254 Pte Tolley to F.A. — N⁰27352 Pte Sandy from F.A.	
	4		N⁰2096 Pte Masters to C.C.S. Company moved to BEAUVAL starting 2-30 a.m. N⁰13553 Pte Rogers R/Base time expired.	
BEAUVAL	5 – 14		Special attention paid to mechanism of VICKERS Guns — open fighting etc. The training included Route Marches — Action from Limbers and also fire control &/c. { T R A H M N G }	
	5		N⁰1435 Corp Bott — N⁰2039 Pte Patterson to F.A. N⁰6856 Pte Heningham to C.C.S.	
	6		N⁰1649 Sgt Mullings to C.C.S. N⁰1435 Corp Bott, N⁰2039 Pte Patterson from F.A.	
	7		N⁰2579 Pte Mahoney to C.C.S	
	8		N⁰9967. Pte Moston to C.C.S Draft of 3 men from CAMIERS allotted 2 to A. 1 to B Section	

Army Form C. 2118.

Machine Gun Company,
144th Infantry Brigade.

WAR DIARY
or
INTELLIGENCE SUMMARY.
(Erase heading not required.)

Instructions regarding War Diaries and Intelligence
Summaries are contained in F. S. Regs., Part II.
and the Staff Manual respectively. Title pages
will be prepared in manuscript.

Place	Date	Hour	Summary of Events and Information	Remarks and references to Appendices
	May			
BEAUVAL	9		No 10097 Pte Quinlan to F.A. No 2386 Pte Cockshill to Cadet School G.H.Q. Leave Party 1 Off. 20 O.R.	57.D.N.2. (3rd photo St)
	10		No 9984 Pte Brown J No 7803 Pte Pritchard to F.A.	
			" " K.C.C.S.	
	14		2/Lt E.J. Bird to M.G.B.D. F.A.	
CORBIE	15		No 2484 Pte Strawbridge K.C.C.S. Company moved with Brigade to BUIRE	
			Went into hut sheds. v C+D Section	
SAILLY	16		Company moved to SAILLY. A.& B. Sections billeted in SAILLY. A.T.B. Sections bow ac bivouaced	C+D Sections Training
			145. Inf. Bde M.G. Coy in trenches East of HEBUTERNE with following dispositions:-	
			WARREN K.21 D.60.55, BRIGGS K.27. D.35.60, HEBUERGEBIRGE K.22.A.15.55, LAFAYETTE K22.B.40.25. PELISSIER K16.A.90.10	
			SQUARE K16.B.10.80. 2 guns in reserve HEBUTERNE	
	17		No 24655 L/Cp Saxton, No 2059 Pte Bryant K.F.A.	
			Guns moved from HEBUTERNE to TURNIER K23.C.25.90. PASTEUR K16.D.6.20.	
	18		No 1462 Pte Gowlin to F.A. Leave party 1 Off 2 O.R.	
	19		No 1959 Pte Lacey to F.A.	
	21		No 1915 Corp Mole to M.G. Grnd CAMIERS No 1643 Pte Pritchard from F.A.	
	22		No 7588 Pte Goode to F.A.	
	23		Sergt A.G. Harris from M.G.C. taken on strength	

Machine Gun Company,
144th Infantry Brigade.

Army Form C. 2118.

WAR DIARY
or
INTELLIGENCE SUMMARY.
(Erase heading not required.)

Place	Date	Hour	Summary of Events and Information	Remarks and references to Appendices
SAULY	1916 May 24		A Section & B Return relieved in trenches by C & D Sections respectively.	A & B Sections Training
	25		No 2959 Pte Bryant from St.A.	
			No 7672 Pte Wallon G.H., No 2259 Pte Bryant to S.A. Enemy artillery active between 10pm & 12 midnight. During which time one m/gun at Spanne & Bhain Traversed	
	26		Enemy barrage. Hostile patrol attempted to cut R.G.H.T. BTN trenches but were driven off with casualties.	
			Enemy bombardment of SAULY. No casualties in Company through B Sections billets were hit.	
	27		No 10097 Pte Quinlan from S.A.	
	29		No 2465 L Cp Carter from S.A. No 1950 Pte Moore Tathealsfrom 1/6 Bn Worcester Regt. No 2313 Pte Burrell to S.A. No 2337 Pte Head W in 1/1K Gloucester Regt	
	30		No 2513 Pte Biss No 2213 Pte Burrell to S.A. No 1919 Pte Goode is attached from 1/4 Gloucester Reg!	
	31		No 1999 Sgt Willis Chackel from 1/8 Worcester Reg!	

[signature]
[signature]
L. GC. 144 M.G. Coy

Confidential

War Diary
Machine Gun Company
144th Infantry Brigade

from 1st June 1916 to 30th June 1916

(Volume 6)

WAR DIARY
or
INTELLIGENCE SUMMARY.

Army Form C. 2118.

.... Brigade.

Instructions regarding War Diaries and Intelligence Summaries are contained in F.S. Regs., Part II. and the Staff Manual respectively. Title pages will be prepared in manuscript.

(Erase heading not required.)

Place	Date	Hour	Summary of Events and Information	Remarks and references to Appendices
SAILLY AU BOIS	1916 June 1		D + C Sections relieved in trenches by 1st & 2nd B.D. Machine Gun Company. Appear Relief complete by 3.30 pm. Company moved to Hebuterne C.o.14.	
"	2		Company moved from C.o.14 at 5 am for BRETEL arriving 10 am. The formation in column of route, of Limbers behind respective Sections was found very trying for the men. An Inspection by C of a few mounts on site. No 1657 Pte Paxton — No 2787 Pte Sidney — No 2267 Pte Symanek 6 P.A, No 2354 Pte Bryant — No 2318 Pte Russell from F.A. No 1657 Pte Paxton — No 2787 Pte Sidney — No 2267 Pte Symanek 6 P.A, No 2354 Pte Bryant — No 2318 Pte Russell from F.A. Cleaning of guns Equipment Limbers — No 21076 Sgt Knight to F.A.	
BRETEL	3			
"	4		Company moved to COULIN VILLERS leaving BRETEL arriving 1pm. Whole company moving in front, of transport from Sabo factory. Lt F.J. Paskin struck off strength Brigade to U.K. sick.	
COULIN VILLERS	5		E Company — Brigade + Divisional Training on SIR C.O. VISER Training area. The chief points brought out were need of extra attention to ① Ammunition Supply	
	6		② Control between Coy H.Q. + Sections ② Sections + Guns.	
			③ Orders + Section Officers being altered by O.C. Battalion + Company Commanders.	
			④ Lack of men i.e. No 5 T.C.	
	12		Ref ① Pack Mule were found very useful turning Preliminary stages when hidden routes not so forward.	
			Ref ② Signal Section increased to 8 instead of 4 authorised.	

Army Form C. 2118.

INTELLIGENCE SUMMARY
or
WAR DIARY

(Erase heading not required.)

Instructions regarding War Diaries and Intelligence Summaries are contained in F. S. Regs., Part II. and the Staff Manual respectively. Title pages will be prepared in manuscript.

Place	Date	Hour	Summary of Events and Information	Remarks and references to Appendices
COURCELLES	1916 June 5.12		Ref No 2. Section Officers warned not to be into using fuses for purposes & in ways contrary to Tactical Usages of the Weapon & such could be possibly awarded without instructing orders of superior officer	
			Ref. note. Report to August H.Q. for 2 men for guns to be attached before any firing action	
	5.17 12.		Moreutz via Strawbridge from C.E.S. Leave party 1 Offr. 20 O.R. Company moved by N.A.R.T.C.M.	
	13		Orghard of Stores & Equipment Company moved to OUTRE-BOIS	
COIGNEUX	14		Company moved to C019 NE 4 u No 37751 Pte J.A. Jones (Saddr) taken on strength Leaving 2 Coys arriving 8 pm	
	15		Cleaning of Guns & Equipment No 21076 Sgt Knight F.W. A.C.C.S. evacuated to England	
	16		Working party of 2 Offrs. H.N.C.O 100 O.R. detailed for loading & unloading work as per B & orders	
	17		" " 1 Off. 2 N.C.O 30 O.R " " " " " "	
	18		" " " 1 N.C.O 12 O.R " " " " " "	
	19		Working parties as day previous	
	20+21+		" " " "	

WAR DIARY or INTELLIGENCE SUMMARY.

Army Form C. 2118.

(Erase heading not required.)

Place	Date	Hour	Summary of Events and Information	Remarks and references to Appendices
COIGNEUX	1916 June 22.		Working Party 1 N.C.O. 100 R. No 21097 Pte Parsons W. 5.C.C.S. broken leg.	
	23.		1 Officer 2 N.C.O's 50 O.R. details for digging Cable Trench in rear of trenches.	
			No 21102. Pte Plant, J. wounded R.S. right shoulder.	
			During the period 17 - 23rd June training which had been arranged could not be properly carried out owing to working parties. Tactical training & preparation of gun equipment etc	
	24.			24 U Day
	25.			25' V.
	26.			26 W
	27th		2/Lieut M.M. Oakford taken on Strength.	27 X
	28th		Cross to Stand by Couselles.	28 Y
	29th		No 3624 Pte Ostrog W + No 8725 Pte Braithwaite taken on Strength.	29 Z
			The following arrangements have been made for forthcoming operations:-	30. A
			2/Lt. Bird OC A Section. Lt. Southam OC C Section Capt Borlase at Bn. H.Q.	B
			Lt. Durant " B. " 2/Lt Harris " D Section Lt. Field to establish forward H.Q.	

Army Form C. 2118.

INTELLIGENCE SUMMARY
or
WAR DIARY
144th Infantry Brigade.

INTELLIGENCE SUMMARY.
(Erase heading not required.)

Instructions regarding War Diaries and Intelligence Summaries are contained in F. S. Regs., Part II. and the Staff Manual respectively. Title pages will be prepared in manuscript.

Place	Date	Hour	Summary of Events and Information	Remarks and references to Appendices
Coigneux	1916 June 30		Lt. Thomas - Lt. Sealman & 2/Lt Oakford will remain with ration dump until required 2/Lt Fry will act as Transport Officer.	
			Owing to shortage of personnel the fact that Company cannot only on obtaining carrying parties from Brigade, except at the very last minute, the question of ammunition supply is very difficult. The following arrangements have been made:—	
			Each section will have a hand cart manned by NCOs when available, with the aid of these it is hoped to establish an ammunition dump forward of Hebuterne & controlled by Forward H.Q.	
			No. 1 & 2 in addition to mount load will carry :- 2 Bandoliers & Extra Water Bottle (emptied and refilled with) Other MGs No. 2 Extra ammunition. Officers NCOs will carry ammunition also.	
			Two shoots for gun will be carried.	

Army Form C. 2118.

WAR DIARY
or
INTELLIGENCE SUMMARY.

Machine Gun Company,
144th Infantry Brigade.

(Erase heading not required.)

Instructions regarding War Diaries and Intelligence Summaries are contained in F.S. Regs., Part II. and the Staff Manual respectively. Title pages will be prepared in manuscript.

Place	Date	Hour	Summary of Events and Information	Remarks and references to Appendices
COIGNEUX & MAILLY-MAILLET	1916 July 1st	8am 9.3am	Zero hour 8am. Company moved with Brigade to Pt. P.18.a. S.W. MAILLY MAILLET. ML reports favorite to complete success of operations by the VIII Corps & it was expected that Division would take over from 107 & 12 Brigade on PUISIEUX ridge as arranged xx During the day the reports were very conflicting till it was apparent that the operations had not been a complete success xx Division HQ 143 Brigade bivouacs at Pt. P.18.a	Ref. 57. D. NE SE 1/20,000
	2nd		Reports that no ground had been gained by VIII Corps confirmed. Orders received that 144 & 145 Brigades & Brigade would attack German front line SgF from Q.10.D.6.7. to Q.18.C.5.2. (12 N. edge of Y RAVINE to NR. THIEPVAL). First three lines to be taken & consolidated xx Object to gain ridge & command Station Road xxx 144 Brigade Centre Right. Brigade left — Brigade right. Time of attack 3.15am 3.7.16 — Order of attack for Brigade 6th Glouc Regt dept Right. 7th Worcester Regt left. 4th Gloucester Regt Brigade Reserve. 8th Worcester Regt Divisional Reserve. One A Section under Lt. Reid to do covering fire — E Section under Lt. Sutton & D Section under Lt. Derrant to go forward with attacking Bns. D Section under Lt. Hayne Brigade Reserve. Ammunition Dump Lt. Field. Division HQ 143 Brigade moved from Pt. P.18.a. Order for attack cancelled after troops were in position. Company returned to Pt. P.18.a. last section reporting	

Army Form C. 2118.

WAR DIARY
or
INTELLIGENCE SUMMARY.
(Erase heading not required.)

Machine Gun Company,
144th Infantry Brigade.

Instructions regarding War Diaries and Intelligence Summaries are contained in F.S. Regs., Part II. and the Staff Manual respectively. Title pages will be prepared in manuscript.

Place	Date	Hour	Summary of Events and Information	Remarks and references to Appendices
MILLY/MAUNET	1916 July 2	6.15 a.m.		
	3		Company moved with Brigade to ob bivouacs at COIGNEUX arriving 7pm.	
			Company moved 6pm to W. SARILL at 10pm & stood to until following morning 8am.	
COURCELLES	4		C Section relieved 93rd Bde M.G. Coy in trenches EAST ST COLINCAMPS } Relief Complete 6.30am. 5.7.16	
			D " " " " " " " " " " " " " " "	
			Dispositions to be organized to be noted.	
	5		Dispositions For G⁰ I E (K34 B55 80) MAITLAND (K34 B35 95) 4 guns in MONK TR.	
			B Kaq Co° 50, K28 D95 95, K28 b 85 05, K268 80 40) TOUVENT FARM (K28 b399) ROSS ACRE	
			Reinforcements some reported (totally untrained). LT SOUTHAM R.F.A. & R.C.L.S	
	6		A Section relieved D Section, B Section relieved C Section relief complete 6.30pm	
	8		A & B Sections relieved by C & D Sections. Moved Emplacement started at TOUVENT FARM	
	9		Telephone installed from Coy H.Q. to Brigade + Coy H.Q. to Central dugout in trenches – This was found extremely useful	
	11		Gun moved from ROSSACRE to No 70 Position (K27 b 7 9)	
	12		A & B Sections relieved C & D Sections, relief complete by 6pm	
	13		Cooperated with artillery + infantry in organized "strafes"	
	14			

Army Form C. 2118.

WAR DIARY
or
INTELLIGENCE SUMMARY.

Machine Gun Company,
144th Infantry Brigade.

(Erase heading not required.)

Instructions regarding War Diaries and Intelligence Summaries are contained in F. S. Regs., Part II. and the Staff Manual respectively. Title pages will be prepared in manuscript.

Place	Date	Hour	Summary of Events and Information	Remarks and references to Appendices
COURCELLES	1916 July 14		Company returned in trenches My E of COLINCAMPS by No115.Coy M.G.C relief complete by	
		11.30pm	Company then moved to BUZINCOURT at 3/7/16 9P.M.	
BUZINCOURT	15.		Company left BOUZINCOURT in Motor Lorries – 1 Son 5.7 T/[?] 12 noon. Company arrived No.s 96 & 97	
			Cops M.G. C in DVILLERS trenches & Relief complete 12 midnight. Disposition as follows:–	
DVILLERS,			DVILLERS (7 guns) 2guns D.Section under Lt Harris between Pts 13 & 104 – 2guns D Sect under Lt THOMAS	
			at Pts 17 & 20. 1gun C Section under Lt THOMAS at S.P63. 2guns L.Section under present disposn at Pt 77.	
			CONISTON ST. A.Section under [?] Bird. 3guns in position for our head fire. 1gun in reserve	
			RYCROFT St. B " – Lt.DUBONT & Lt. SOLIMAN 2guns in support but positions	
			DORSET St. 1 Gun B-Section. 1gun C.Section	
			Transport HEDAUVILLE. Pers in COURS.	
	Night of 16/17		See Appendix 1. [?] day of 4. Guiszelli party [?]	
	17.		During hours of DVILLERS & a forward advance organised & commenced at 4.30pm by 1/4 R. Wores Regt	
			& THOMAS 1/2 NOTBth Guns moved with 4th Supported left flank 3rd Hussar moved with & supported right	
			flank. Also 3 guns CSection under Pat OXFORD went to a position between Pt 15 & Pt 33 as reserve.	
		6.30pm	At 6.30pm DORSETS moved forward with 2/3 10/12 guns A Support Centre.	
			Lieut CRUICKSHANK seven along East Brightly Pts as. 46 – 88 – 98 – 16 with Buckinghams &	

NB. 4 guns was 1/5000 special map will pencil changes enclosed.

T2131. Wt. W708–776. 500000. 4/15. Sir J. C. & S.

Army Form C. 2118.

WAR DIARY
or
INTELLIGENCE SUMMARY.
(Erase heading not required.)

Machine Gun Company,
144th Infantry Brigade.

Place	Date	Hour	Summary of Events and Information	Remarks and references to Appendices
OVILLERS	1916 July 17		4 Lewis Guns forward. Four Guns Came into action in this line. Lt THOMAS i/c N° 13 & 14 Gun in position near Pt 46 & 2/Lieut BAMFORD i/c N° 10 & 12 Gun between Pts 46 & 88. 2/Lieut HAYNE brought N° 11 & 15 & 16 Guns into action at N.E. Corner of OVILLERS towards right flank + junction of Brigades. During the night 17/18 N° 12 Gun was buried by shell fire & the team killed wounded or buried. Sgt Toombs 1/7th Bn. Wa. R.I att. M.G.Coy & 2/Lieut OAKFORD showed great coolness + gallantry – specially Oakford who dug out 6 wounded men under intense shellfire & returned afterwards to dig out the gun. Killed { N° 22557 L/Cpl Dinwell, N° 22257 Pte Hammond J., N° 2256 Pte Culverf. } Wounded N° 1246 Pte Booth – Shell Shock N° 9815 Pte Windsor.	All refs. 1/100 Special map with points already marked.
	18th		During the period 15/18 July 1916 two forward wires were brought out. 1. The necessity for keeping Guns in posn under Officers sight during operations of this type when through in "trenches" more than one movement. 2. The necessity in fighting of this nature when Ts a Forward H.Q. to control relays in touch with forward guns "O.C." Forward Munch. This forward H^{t}Q ought to be in close touch with Bg H.Q. by telephone + runners + in touch with forward Guns by runner. Forward HQ established with telephone to runners to Coy HQ – N° 13 & 16 Guns under 2/Lieut Haine moved to position between Pts 88 & 85. Following relief also took place: 2/Lieut Bird with N° 11 & 12 Guns	

WAR DIARY or INTELLIGENCE SUMMARY

Army Form C. 2118.

Machine Gun Company,
143rd Infantry Brigade.

Place	Date	Hour	Summary of Events and Information	Remarks and references to Appendices
OVILLERS	1916 July 18	X	Lt THOMAS & No.3 13th Guns at P.7.4.6. No.3 Gun going to forward H.Q. & echelon No.9 Gun. 2/Lieut Dalziel with No.5 9710 Guns returned to CONNISTON ST. Lt Durrant with No.8 Gun moved up to forward H.Q. Giving 2 Guns in action. Wounded No.2287 Pte Gerrard M.G.C.	
	18/19		2/Lieut Bird cooperates with 1/7th Warwickshire Regt ? in attack, moving his Guns forward in close support – No.19 3/9 Corp Reed again showed great coolness & initiative. The attack was unsuccessful & guns were moved back to original positions. No.1 Gun knocked out during heavy shelling. The necessity for gun being well away from trenches was brought out.	
	19	X	Positions were made with special supervision of Officers Brig. See Appendix 2	
			Lt SELLMAN with No.7 & 8 Guns relieves the HAMEL & No.13 & 16 Guns – these Guns returned to Reserve Coy HQ. Lt Durrant with No.5 STB. 1 Gun Relief. 1 Gun E Section between Pts 11.39 Forward H.Q. Guns carried out on positions the between Pts 11.39 P.7.4.6 No.2089 Pte Bryant 1/4/16 Gun R.17 AT M.G.C. Wounded No 15710 Pte ... M.G.C.	
	20.		Lt SELLMAN & No.7 & 8 Guns moved to positions taken P.7.4.4 to cooperate with 1/8th Regt. "1 hour in attack & to meet forward if attack was successful No.2294 A/Corp Macbride showed great devotion to duty, also No 21719 St Lyons attacked not successful & Guns moved back to "P.7.8.S" Roy Gun was buried & No.14 311 Pte Frank R.E. wounded. No 1835 Cpl Marston U.S.B. Donn & No 2313 Pte Reeve showed great coolness & devotion & duty. No 1635 Cpl Martin Shellshock	
	21		Lt THOMAS No.13 & 14 Guns relieves Lt Sellman & No.7 & 8 Guns. 2/Lt HAIME E relieved 2/Lt Bird & No 10 & 12 Guns	
	22/23		No.5 Guns returned to CONNISTON ST. Reserve at Coy HQ. See Appendix 3	

WAR DIARY
or
INTELLIGENCE SUMMARY.
(Erase heading not required.)

Army Form C. 2118.

Machine Gun Company,
144th Infantry Brigade.

Place	Date	Hour	Summary of Events and Information	Remarks and references to Appendices
OUVILLERS	1916 July 23rd	x	2/Lt OXFORD Nr 10 M 71 relieves Lt DURANT Nr 5 M 5 guns. Nr 9 Gun Bivous 15 Bowers H.Q. Wounded Nr D 1760 Pte Bridge G.R.	
	24		1.15 Run Pte Present arrived from taken in Strongpoint Bay Pte Byrd Shot to will his gun which had been moved from 15 to H.Q. owing to attempted enemy attack by enemy whilst horses were staked by 7 M.R. Bn. Shouts No 74 Gun under Cpl Hale started evening a stanching along shallow trench to trench loops over one night. This party was disposed of fire maintained on trench for 3hrs through position was being continually shelled. At 6.30 pm all guns registered on German front line. During resultant shelling Nr 16 Gun was knocked out Nr 19 D Pte Proud wounded from F.A. Nr 4885 Pte Wakely to M.H. Nr 8499 Bmd. W. Nr 22583 — Moon D.J.	Guns in connection M. maintained fire on line Nr 22, 23, 65, 76, 96, 04, 407
	25		Gun at Pt 85 disposed numerous parties during the day which were endeavouring to cross. Gun party was heavily disposed but 2 or 3 new killed at a range of 2100 yds. The Pte Bird with Nr 172 Guns relieved 1 gun of Nr 3rd B.H. at Pt 78 and Nr 13 gun at Pt 444. Lt THOMAS relieved Lt DURANT Mr.	S. 6. 8
	26		Firing from Pt. 85 continued during the day. Lt SKELLMAN with Nr 1 gun relieves Lt HARRIS + Nr 12.15.16 Guns. Lt DURANT & Nr 7 gun relieves Lt THOMAS exp. 13 gun at 3 H.Q.	

Army Form C. 2118.

WAR DIARY
or
INTELLIGENCE SUMMARY

Machine Gun Company, 3 144th Infantry Brigade.

(Erase heading not required.)

Instructions regarding War Diaries and Intelligence Summaries are contained in F. S. Regs., Part II. and the Staff Manual respectively. Title Pages will be prepared in manuscript.

Place	Date	Hour	Summary of Events and Information	Remarks and references to Appendices
Ovillers–Bouzincourt, Hédauville, Arquèves–Beauval, Franqueville	1916 July 27		During period 15/7/16 July – 27th July foot work was done by No.10 Sec. Coy. S.M. Nicholl Bouzincourt	
			Company relieved in trenches by 10/37 Coy. M.G.C. & moved back to Transport lines & thence to Hédauville. Lt Thomas R.T.A.	
	28.		Company moved with Brigade from Hédauville to Arquèves { Guns & Personnel departure 7.46 am, arrival 10.15 am; Trans. & Personnel departure 7.33 am, arrival 10.30 am.	
	29.		Arquèves to Beauval. departure 4.32 am, arrival 10 a.m.	
	30.		Beauval to Franqueville	
			2/Lieut Clutton R.T. taken on strength with 11 reinforcements. 2/Lieut Clutton posted to A Section.	
Franqueville	31.		Cleaning of Guns & equipment.	
			Remarks	
			1/ Continuous march route negligible owing to shortage of men on Guns which meant that to take teams which could be made.	
			2/ Signal section totally inadequate (1 N.C.O. + 3 men to 4 telephones) – No provision made in establishment for runners.	
			3/ Great tendency for Guns working in Bde. areas to be too much at the beck call of Bde officers. This is due to Shortage of personnel for control (ie Shortage of Signallers & runners) & is liable to cause contradictory orders & the main scheme of defence or attack as ordered by OC Coy being seriously affected.	

Sample of temporary M.G. emplacement.

Plan

Section.

covered (for sentry)
gun platform
fire step
well forward

APPENDIX 2

Plans of temporary M.G. Emplacement made with fraised of trench occupied.

This emplacement was made of parados of captured enemy trench, smashed by shell fire, by joining a series of shell holes. It was ready for occupation after one night's work by one team, and completely finished the next. Covered portion was made of 9 foot pieces of timber, found on the spot, & earth, & was intended as splinter-proof for sentry. Gun was also kept under it by day. Emplacement was frequently fired from and was undamaged by three heavy bombardments. Previously, two guns had been destroyed, three men killed & four wounded in two days, while gun position was in trench.

Sample of temporary M.G. emplacement.

Plan.

(diagram: Very wide trench with sap about 2'0" wide, covered portion, fire steps, 4'×4' gun platform (sandbagged))

Section.

(diagram: covered (for sentry), gun platform, fire step)

This emplacement was made well forward of parados of captured enemy trench, smashed by shell fire, by joining a series of shell holes. It was ready for occupation after one nights work by one team, and completely finished the next. Covered portion was made of stout pieces of timber, found on the spot, & earth, & was intended as splinterproof for sentry. Gun was also kept under it by day. Emplacement was frequently fired from and was undamaged by three heavy bombardments. Previously, two guns had been destroyed, three men killed & four wounded in two days, while gun position was in trench.

R.M.Lidbett
14th Machine Gun Coy

Army Form C. 2118.

144th Infantry Brigade.

WAR DIARY
or
INTELLIGENCE SUMMARY
(Erase heading not required.)

Instructions regarding War Diaries and Intelligence Summaries are contained in F. S. Regs., Part II. and the Staff Manual respectively. Title Pages will be prepared in manuscript.

Place	Date	Hour	Summary of Events and Information	Remarks and references to Appendices
FRANQUE VILLE	1916 August 1		No 8999 Pte Bond to Hosp JA. — No 2187 McKeown ATA	Cleaning of Guns, Limbers Equipment etc:
	2		2/Lieut W H Green — Lieut E J Haggard Taken on Strength.	Gun drill.
	4		No 2189 Pte Kenwin from JA.	Classes in Mechanism & Gun Action etc
	5		Capt H. P. Barlow to JA.	For reinforcements.
			Inspection by B.G. Comdg	
	9		Company marched with Brigade to AUTHIEUX via THIENVILLERS	
	10		No 2176S Pte Gunn away to JA.	PUCHVILLERS via BEAUVAL & BEAUQUESNE
	11		No 2287 Pte Smith Z — No 2157 Pte Kenwin to JA.	
	12		Company moved with Brigade to BOUZINCOURT via TOUTENCOURT — HARPONVILLE — HEDAUVILLE No 2179 Pte Mahony Taken on Strength No 2857, 3 Pte Rim — No 2059 Pte Bryant from CCS.	
			No 2176 Pte Burke to No 4306 Pte Cumberson to JM	
	13		Company relieved 37th M G Coy in OVILLERS Trenches — No Casualties	
			Dispositions as follows:—	

WAR DIARY or INTELLIGENCE SUMMARY

144th Infantry Brigade

Army Form C. 2118.

Place	Date	Hour	Summary of Events and Information	Remarks and references to Appendices
OVILLERS	1916 Aug 13.		C Section Section HQ CONISTON.	
			D – + 1 Team B. Section in trench OVILLERS POST.	
			OVILLERS + trenches North of OVILLERS	
			A Section { 1 Gun S Pt 16 N. Corner of Village A Section 2 Guns Section HQ E + W of Pt 46.	
			1 Gun . 44 (X 2 D) (X 8 a)	
			A Section 2 Guns Section HQ in trench between Pts 11 & 39 (X 2 c) 1 Gun Local supports Pts (X 8 c)	
			Company HQ OVILLERS Post Forward Company HQ Pt 26. (X 8 C)	
		13/14.	Lt Sellman + No 22294 Sergt Mockett led by Brigade on right & small footing in it.	
		14	Enemy Counter attacks SKYLINE TR – M.G. Cover CAMIERS	
		14/5	Enemy's trenches searched Continuous by Stoney Jay.	
			Cooperated with 6th Glo: Regt in attack on Pts 44, 55, 62, 23 (X 2 D)	
			Two guns under 2/Lieut Bird moved forward to Pt 47 (X 2 D). 54 these enf ar covering attacks, flanking fire to the attacks & the other was kept ready to move forward to further attacks	
			Captures. M.G. barrage was also maintained on supports & communications in rear. Sgt Bolt. Cpl Reade + Pte Dixon did good work. Attacks unsuccessful & guns
			withdrawn to original positions. No 15595 Pte Payne KCCI

WAR DIARY or INTELLIGENCE SUMMARY

144th Infantry Brigade

Place	Date	Hour	Summary of Events and Information	Remarks and references to Appendices
OVILLERS	1916 Aug 15		No 21059 Sgt Byun. No 21586 Corp Waldron No 21681 A/Sgt Bearn to Cadet School G.H.Q. No 20159 Pte Bryant accidentally wounded.	
	15/16		Good results were obtained from fire on various parties of the Enemy. Co-operated with 4th Glos Regt in attack on Pts 74, 62, 20. M.G. barrage maintained in support + Communication Trenches in rear. Attack unsuccessful.	
	16		Company relieved by 143 M.G.Coy & returned to Bilittes Bouzincourt. No 21762 Pte Burke } Concussion No 4308 } BCSS	
	17		Cleaning up of Guns and Equip used + inspection by section officers. 2/Lieut Chitter } transferred 2/Lieut Green } 5/145 M.G.Coy	
	17/18		Company stood to from 12 mid night until 2.30 a.m.	
	18		Company stood to from 4 p.m. C & D Sections moved to DURANT wood up to OVILLERS with 4 Glos Regt in Support 143 Brigade of necessary 2/Lieut Bird with M.G.Coy as Second in Command.	
	19		Relieved 14.55 M.G.Coy. with disposition as under:— C Section 2 Guns Pt 89 (X36) 1 Gun Pt 99 (X32) 1 Gun across Cy HQ D Section 2" Pt 94 (X26) 1" Pt 48 (X96) 1 Gun – Cy HQ Arto Section RESERVE at LAKE VIEW (M25 A)	

WAR DIARY or INTELLIGENCE SUMMARY

(Erase heading not required.)

144th Infantry Brigade

Place	Date	Hour	Summary of Events and Information	Remarks and references to Appendices
OVILLERS	1916 Aug. 20		General re-adjustment of line – 144 Inf Bde taking over command of whole line occupied by the Division including 143 M.G. Coy in disposition as held by 144 M.G. Coy on 13th inst. + No.4 Batt. M.M.G. + 4 Hotchkiss Guns of Yorkshire Yeomanry. Two guns under Lieut. Harris moved from Pt 94 (X2B) to Pt 44 (X2B) from which position direct enfilade of enemy trenches in ZEALOUS SALIENT was obtained. Arrangements made with O.E. 143 M.G. Coy - O.C. No. 4 Batt. M.M.Gs + O.C. Hotchkiss Guns to have co-operation + centralisation of control. Brigade HQ (BONNET POST) Company HQ OVILLERS POST, 7p. Coy HQ Pt 26 Transport lines shelled – No 22303 Pte Phipps wounded. 1 horse wounded. Capt A.P. Bastow struck off strength Co-operated with B.15 Gp + 7/Worcester in attack on line Pts 31-79-91-20 (R31C+X2A) to England	
	21		Barrage maintained on enemy support & communication trenches especially in R31.D. No 37999 Pte Davison wounded. No 4306 Pte Cumperson from C.C.S. Bertinee 12 noon. Cooperated with 4th Glos + 6th Glos in attack on line R32C15. R31A81-X1B18-X1A98 R31C90 62-84. Guns registered by direct observation were so disposed as to directly enfilade enemy support and communication trenches in area of attack. During operations hostile troops retiring and also attempting barrage were observed & were held up by the fire with good results. 2 co lines from	
	22		A Selection relieved B Section - B Selection relieved C Section. Fire maintained on enemy trenches – (good) results obtained. No A2938 Pte Evry J. wounded	
	23		Brigade relieved by 145 Bde + 25 Division – B Section relieved by 143 M.G. Coy.	

Army Form C. 2118.

WAR DIARY or INTELLIGENCE SUMMARY

(Erase heading not required.)

144th Infantry Brigade.

Instructions regarding War Diaries and Intelligence Summaries are contained in F. S. Regs., Part II. and the Staff Manual respectively. Title Pages will be prepared in manuscript.

Place	Date	Hour	Summary of Events and Information	Remarks and references to Appendices
OVILLERS	1916 Aug. 23.		Remainder of Company remained in position co-operated with 145 Inf. Bde. in attack on Pts 79-29 & Pts 79-34. (R2A & R3aC). Good results were again obtained & A & B Sections relieved by 145 M.G. Coy. - Company returned to Bullets Bzin-Bori.	
	24.		2/Lt. A.L.N. Jennings taken on strength.	
	25.		No. 42437 Pte Scott J. No. 21080 Pte Andrews M. No. 21096 Pte Mincher W. S.F.A.	
FORCEVILLE	26.		Company marched Bullets FORCEVILLE.	
ENGLE BELMER	27.		Company relieved 71st M.G. Coy & 162 M.G. Coy in BEAUMONT HAMEL trenches. Dispositions as under. Coy H.Q. ENGLEBELMER.	
			C Section 2 Guns Fort ANLEY. Q15.A 90.05 2 guns local support ENGLEBELMER	
			A Section 4 guns in line Q15.690.40 - Q16.C 3.7. Q16.C.9.4 Q10.C.98	
			B Section 4 Guns in line Q15.A.80.25 Q10.B.1.5. Q4.C.9.75. Q4A.95.25	
			D Section 2 Guns THE BOWERY Q3.D.90.60 Q3.A.35.10 2 " local support AUCHONVILLERS	
			No 3 M.G. Batt. 3 guns AUCHONVILLERS defence positions.	
MAILLY MAILLET	28		Company H.Q moved to MAILLY-MAILLET.	
	30.		Lt. BOTHWICK reports to Command.	
	31st		C Section relieves A Section - A Section relieves D Section	

WAR DIARY
or
INTELLIGENCE SUMMARY

(Erase heading not required.)

Instructions regarding War Diaries and Intelligence Summaries are contained in F.S. Regs., Part II. and the Staff Manual respectively. Title Pages will be prepared in manuscript.

Place	Date	Hour	Summary of Events and Information	Remarks and references to Appendices
MAILLY-MAILLET	1916 Aug 31		During this period a shortage in establishment either work on officers & men which is establishment causes. This shortage entails extra work on officers & men which is detrimental to efficiency in the long run. The Company returns was received by a large number of M.G. Coys during the period & in no case was a Company's strength normally less than 200. The & cers on establishment was made up with men attached from units in Brigade. It would appear that either establishment should be increased or that official authority should be given for attachment of men from units in Brigade.	

A.H. Webb
Major
O/c Company,
Cmdg. Machine Gun Company,
144th Infantry Brigade

Confidential

War Diary

Vol 9

of

144 Machine Gun Company

from 1st September 1916 to 30th September 1916

Volume 9

2449 Wt. W14957/M90 750,000 1/16 J.B.C. & A. Forms/C.2118/12.

WAR DIARY
or
INTELLIGENCE SUMMARY Machine Gun Company,
144th Infantry Brigade.
(Erase heading not required.)

Place	Date	Hour	Summary of Events and Information	Remarks and references to Appendices
MAILLY-MAILLET	1916 Sept 1		Reinforcements. No 43459 Pte Cork taken on strength. Lt. BORTHWICK left to command 144 M.G. Coy. Lt. ASHINDEN returned to be attached to 144 M.G.Coy. No 21050 Pte Holmes to C.C.S. Weather conditions fine and trenches dry.	
	2		Three guns fired on enemy's wire throughout the night. Preparation for cooperation with 39th Division. Orders as under:— No 1 & 3 M.G.'s to cooperate the fire of 3 Guns on "Y" Ravine — 2 Guns to Gun left flank of attack with direct fire onto enemy parapets & communications — 2 Guns, indirect fire down STATION ROAD. 4 Guns to search ground in and behind BEAUMONT HAMEL — 4 Guns to take part in feint on BEAUMONT HAMEL TRs.	
	3	5.10 am	Zero time 5.10 am. M.G. fire maintained as ordered, but owing to mist and smoke no observation obtained. Enemy shelled Right Sector fairly heavily. Lewis teams outposts maintained fire any failure of enemy attack intervene-fell. No 43636 Pte Watson W. to C.C.S. No 22289 Pte Smith No 2167 Pte Brown to C.C.S. No 43442 Cpl Mitchell taken on strength. 1/16 section relief	
	4	8.30 pm	Guns changed at 8.30 pm. M.G.'s searched enemy trenches. Enemy shelling fairly heavy intermittently on Right Sub Section when 2 guns of D Section were temporarily put out of action owing to teams being buried by shell fire.	
	5		B&D Sections relieved by 145 M.G. Coy and returned to billets MAILLY. - MAILLY - MAILLET	

WAR DIARY
or
INTELLIGENCE SUMMARY

(Erase heading not required.)

Machine Gun Company,
144th Infantry Brigade.

Place	Date	Hour	Summary of Events and Information	Remarks and references to Appendices
MAILLY-MAILLET	1916. Sept 6		A.T.C. Section ordered by 117 M.G. Coy. Company moved to Hutments Bois de WARNIMONT No 1838 Pte Martin I.A. taken on the Strength	
	7.		Cleaning of Guns Equipment and Training	
	8.		Do do	
	9.		Inspection by G.O.C. 48th Division	
	10.		Cleaning of Guns & Equipment. No 21079 Pte Winterbottom Leave U.K.	
	11.		Company moved to Hutments Bus.	
	12.		Do Training	
	13.		Company moved to BARLIER & from there back to BARTON	
	14.		Training — chiefly of an Elementary nature	
	15.			
	17.			
	14.		No 7589 Pte Mann & 32554 Cpl Saddler to CCS	
	15.		No 16792 Pte Walter 22298 Pte Twins & 2864 Pte Jenkins CCS No 20059 Pte Bryant taken on Strength No 18 reports to Sanitary work went sick base to U.K.	
	18.		Company moved to AUTHEUX	

WAR DIARY
or
INTELLIGENCE SUMMARY

Machine Gun Company,
144th Infantry Brigade.

(Erase heading not required.)

Place	Date	Hour	Summary of Events and Information	Remarks and references to Appendices
RUTHEUX	1916 Sep 19			Training - Practices on 30 & 600 yd Range. Combined work with infantry. Visual training & taking orders work. Inoculation of Coy.
	20		No 21082 Sgt Barclay No 21092 Pte Hawkes to FA	
	21		No 42950 Pte Hastings to FA	
	22		No 21082 Sgt Barclay No 21451 Pte Hollingworth No 21092 Pte Hawkes No 42950 Pte Hastings C.O.S.	
	23		No 42957 Pte Elliot RTA	
	25		2nd Lt M G Evans Courses	
	28		Brigade day - Exercise to bring out March Discipline Approach to attack - attack of village, & taking up of line on far side.	
	30		Company moved with Brigade to IVERGNY.	

[signature] Capt.
144 M.G. Coy
1.10.16

Confidential

Vol 10

War Diary

of

144 Machine Gun Company

from 1st October 1916 to 31st October 1916

Volume 10

2449 Wt. W14957/M90 750,000 1/16 J.B.C. & A. Forms/C.2118/12.

Army Form C. 2118.

WAR DIARY
or
INTELLIGENCE SUMMARY

Machine Gun Company,
144th Infantry Brigade.

(Erase heading not required.)

Instructions regarding War Diaries and Intelligence Summaries are contained in F. S. Regs., Part II. and the Staff Manual respectively. Title Pages will be prepared in manuscript.

Place	Date	Hour	Summary of Events and Information	Remarks and references to Appendices
	1916 October			
IVERGNY to GRENAS	1		Company moved with Brigade to GRENAS.	
GRENAS	2		No 22554 Cpl Sadler J. from C.C.S. No 33634 A/Cpl Robson - No 43655 Pte Mackenzie - No 53649 Pte Davis from Base Depot.	
	3		No 22292 Pte Brown to 7/R. No 22957 Pte Willett K.C.E.S.	
	7		No 22292 Pte Brown from F.A.	
	2		Company expects to go into the line at short notice & training consists chiefly in the instruction of chaps in Mechanism etc. The preparation etc of all gun Equipment for trenches - Short Route Marches & daily training of Lewis Section	
	8			
	9		C Section relieves Section of 143 M.G.Coy in FONQUEVILLERS trenches.	
Fm. de la BREFFAYE	10		Company moved to Fm de la BREFFAYE. No 21066 Pte Clark G. F.A. - C.C.S. (11.10.16)	
	13		B Section relieved C Section in the line. C Section returning to Fm. de la BREFFAYE	
	14		D Section relieved 145 M.G.Coy in HEARTHERNE trenches.	
SOUASTRE	15		Company HQ moved to SOUASTRE No 22713 Pte Trod - No 42948 Pte Jeffray A. No 22565 Pte Wood E.J. to F.A. No 21762 Pte Banks to F.A. No 22297 Pte Strawbridge dose E S.V.R.	

2449 Wt. W14957/M90 750,000 1/16 J.B.C. & A. Forms/C.2118/12.

Army Form C. 2118.

WAR DIARY
or
INTELLIGENCE SUMMARY
Machine Gun Company,
144th Infantry Brigade.

(Erase heading not required.)

Instructions regarding War Diaries and Intelligence Summaries are contained in F. S. Regs., Part II. and the Staff Manual respectively. Title Pages will be prepared in manuscript.

Place	Date	Hour	Summary of Events and Information	Remarks and references to Appendices
HANNESCAMP SOUASTRE	1916 Oct 17.		A Section relieved B Section in the line. No 22525 Pte Noone to C.C.S.	
HEBUTHERNE	18.		A & D Sections relieved so 15 M.G Coy on their right in HEBUTHERNE. Transln. Company H.Q. moved to HEBUTHERNE. No 22289 Pte Snell L. No 30832 Pte Colman to Army Sport	
	19.		C & B Sections moved to SAILLY - A.M Shien & transport to SOUASTRE	
	20.		C & B Section moved to IVERGNY. Company relieved in the line by 148 M.G Coy & moved to SOUASTRE	
IVERGNY	21.		H.Q. & ½ Company moved to IVERGNY. No 2713 Pte Thul H. to C.C.S. 2/Lieut D. Hur to GRANTHAM (A.G. 9/8864) No 21762 Pte Burbee to C.C.S. 32 men taken on strength from Base in Brigade.	No 48816 Pte Wilks No 23573 Pte Brown 5.7 PM
	22.			
	23.		These men were allotted in the following way :- Each Section was made up to 2 Sgts 2 Cpls & 24 S/afu & Ptes. The remaining men were taken to a H.Q. Section - with the following objects in view. Firstly in order to keep the Sections Strength as nearly uniform as possible by attaching men from HQ Section to replace Sick or Casualties when they occur —	

2449 Wt. W14957/M90 759,000 1/16 J.B.C. & A. Forms/C.2118/12.

INTELLIGENCE SUMMARY

**Machine Gun Company,
144th Infantry Brigade.**

(Erase heading not required.)

Place	Date	Hour	Summary of Events and Information	Remarks and references to Appendices
IVERGNY	1916 Oct 23		instead of mere allotting all men to Section & having perhaps large gaps in some Sections & not in others, owing to Sections casualties lost being unknown. Secondly in order to have a small body of men available for return carrying. "Runners – Pioneer work in trenches etc:– Thus giving a more complete roll to half Company out of the line. It is proposed to pass all reinforcements through this H.Q Section before allotting them to Sections & to allow Sections to return unless Gunners to this Section to be refined by better Gunners. Also Range Finders will be kept with this Section (until 1 instrument per Section is available) & will be sent out to Sections when required – this should be beneficial to the instruments as they will not always be in the line. In cases when a forward dump of ammunition is required there men will be very useful & also when any Section wishes an ammunition carrier for any special reason. The increase of the Establishment by 32 men & the transport makes the organising working & control of a Machine Gun Company possible – but 20 to 30 men Extra are still required in order to make a Machine Gun Company a complete & thoroughly efficient Unit	

INTELLIGENCE SUMMARY

Machine Gun Company, 144th Infantry Brigade.

(Erase heading not required.)

Place	Date	Hour	Summary of Events and Information	Remarks and references to Appendices
IVERGNY & BRESLE	1916 Oct 24		Transport moved with Brigade Group to IVERGNY and dismounted portion stood by to move in buses to BRESLE on 25th. The period under review has been very unsettled – more have been frequent & organised continuous Training has been difficult. The location of Officers being recalled to GRANTHAM + posted to other Companies has caused great difficulties. In the case of this Machine Gun Company 2/Lieut Ibis was recalled to GRANTHAM, at a time when the change of Transport Officer was liable to be unsettling. Another officer with as much experience in its Field and more Experience on the Gun Guts more easily have been Spared. Also 2/Lieut Ed Bird transferred from this Company as 2nd Second i/c of the 15th M.G.Cy was not given the appointment with that Company – took over a Strange Section on joining into a Sgcf over the head of the former Section officer, while the section he commanded here went into a Sgcf in another part of the line also under a strange officer. The efficiency of two Sections being thus impaired at critical periods.	
	25 — 30		Training. Including:-Training of Reinforcements from Battalions Use of Compass for night marching Use of Pack mules.	
ALBERT	31.		Company moved with Brigade to ALBERT	

H. Webb Capt.
Cmdg. Machine Gun Company,
144th Infantry Brigade.

WAR DIARY or INTELLIGENCE SUMMARY

Machine Gun Company,
144th Infantry Brigade.

Place	Date	Hour	Summary of Events and Information	Remarks and references to Appendices
ALBERT	1916 Nov. 1		Preparation for trenches.	
BAZENTIN LE PETIT	2		Company relieved 4th R.W.K. Coy in Lo Sars trenches. The dispositions:— 1 Gun M.22.b.35.15. 1 Gun M.22.b.05.05. } Section H.Q. 1 Gun M.21.b.91.25. 1 Gun M.22.c.8.6. } M.22.b.05.95. 1 Gun M.16.b.4.7. 1 Gun M.16.b.2.0. } Section H.Q. 1 Gun M.16.a.55.05. 1 Gun Bazentin le Petit Cemetery. } Section H.Q. Pte Cutting Le Sars. M/S T.M. Stores Argentin Le Petit Cemetery	Mr S Wickens — C.Y. H.Q. + Transport + R.M.S. Stores Argentin Le Petit Cemetery
	3		M/S 10305 Pte Answard K.O.C.S. Company HQ + remaining teams of C Section moved to Martin Puich also hut H.H.R. Section Le Sars Cemetery. Transport + a.m.s stores to Bde Transport lines Becourt. Gun maintained on trucks in M.10 - M.11. B Section relieved C Section in Le Sars.	
MARTINPUICH	4		Co-operated with 50 M.G.Coy in our single attack counterattack — supporting new attack on the Butte with Flanking fire.	
	5		Sgt Harris did extremely fine work on this occasion after the Sergeant was killed + Gunner. M/S 11330 Pte Cochran again showed great coolness + endurance. Casualties 2 Lt Q.J. Haggard killed No 2038 Pte Davis " No 20294 Pte Ash wounded No 15730 Pte Battees No 4385 Mathews No 37987 Gorham Shell Shock	

WAR DIARY
or
INTELLIGENCE SUMMARY

Machine Gun Company
144th ...

Place	Date	Hour	Summary of Events and Information	Remarks and references to Appendices
MARTINPUICH	1916 Nov 6		During heavy shelling before and after German counter attack the Company had the following Casualties:- Killed No 20375 Pte Stephens, No 14,619 Pte Patterson. Wounded No 24467 Pte Acheson, No 9728 Pte Jones at duty. Shell shock - Lt. Thomas & 3 O.R. to M.G. Course. {Relieved B Section, D " " C Section}	
	7			
	8		Section returned. Relieved with out hitch.	
	10		R.O. Section relieved A & D Sections. Reinforcements 15 O.R.	
	11		Company (less ½ Section (B+C) relieved_by_the which took over Capt Mort relieved by 1½ M.G. Coy. Sections relieved in the line - 2 Bayentin, ½(C.Sect)Lonely Trench Camp. No 25114 Pte Torno G wounded.	
	12		½ Company to Lonely Trench Camp. During this period the Conditions were extremely difficult & new Guns out of the line absolutely "done up". It would have been impossible to carry on with out the R.R. Section as carrying parties & the scheme of a 5th Section proved its worth. In not only could Ample Ammunition have ration carried up to them - but casualties were	

WAR DIARY
or
INTELLIGENCE SUMMARY

Machine Gun Company,
144th Infantry Brigade.

(Erase heading not required.)

Instructions regarding War Diaries and Intelligence Summaries are contained in F. S. Regs., Part II. and the Staff Manual respectively. Title Pages will be prepared in manuscript.

Place	Date	Hour	Summary of Events and Information	Remarks and references to Appendices
LONEY IR. Camp	1916 Nov			
	12		immediately replaced without drawing on other sections. The point was again brought out very strongly – i.e. the smallness of the number of boots allowed on stock. (6)	
	13		Reinforcements to S.R.	
	14		3 O.R. to S.R. 2 O.R. from S.R.	
MARTINPUICH	15		A & B Sections relieved 3 "nests" in Corps line held by No 5 M.G.Cy & went into by them each of A + C Sections – these teams returning to Lonely Trench Camp. Coy H.Q. to MARTIN PUICH.	
	17		A + B Sections relieved 3 O.R. to R.C.E.S.	
	31		No. 5 M.G.Cy relieved D Section in Corps line – B Section relieved No 9 M.G.Cy in trenches opposite THE BUTTE dispositions	
			1 Gun MAXWELL M.17 c 6.9. 1 Gun — THE SIMPLE M.16 d 9.5. ⎫ Relieve 1/2	
			1 Gun THE IVES. M.17 c 10 U.5. 1 Gun SHEPHERD M.22 b 9.5. ⎬ THE SPING M.17 c 5.4.	
			RIGHT H.Q. M.23 b1 M	
			Casualties No 20713 Pte Osborne A. Drowning	
	19		Pte. Pemberton G. taken on Strength	

WAR DIARY
or
INTELLIGENCE SUMMARY

Machine Gun Company, 144th Infantry Brigade

(Erase heading not required.)

Place	Date	Hour	Summary of Events and Information	Remarks and references to Appendices
MAROIX in Front	1916 Nov 24		The relief was carried out under extremely trying conditions and officers & OR are to be congratulated on the discipline & endurance meanwhile shown.	
	25		Company arrived in billets at SNELLIER WOOD. To FA. 15R. From FA. 20R.	
	26. 27		Lt OAKFORD 2nd R ATM G Course. Lt E.M THOMAS to S.O M G Coy as 2 i/c & to Corps ATM 878. 30R to FA.	
	29		Officers 3 OR leave U.K.	
			The month under review has been the most trying since the formation of the Company & it has only been possible by the splendid spirit shown by all ranks & Huns have been forced — for men in a trenches who at least for times in this long as those done by Infantry. The appointment of a Corps M.G.O will do much to improve conditions & facilitate the working of Machine Gun Companies. As also regards AM.R.T & G branches and supplies a long felt need — Owing as it does an interesting liason M.G Coys The Base and an Expert of Lewis Rank on the spot to whom difficulties can be submitted.	

P.R. Fub Capt.
Cmdg. Machine Gun Company,
144th Infantry Brigade.

Vol 12

Confidential

War Diary
of
144 Machine Gun Company

from 1st December/16 to 31st December/16

Volume 12

WAR DIARY
or
INTELLIGENCE SUMMARY

Machine Gun Company,
144th Infantry Brigade.

Army Form C. 2118.

Place	Date	Hour	Summary of Events and Information	Remarks and references to Appendices
1916 Dec. SHELTER WOOD	1916 Dec. 1		Preparation for trenches. 22546 Cpl Wall 22294 Cpl Mackrell } C.C.S.	
MARTINPUICH	2		Coy relieved 143 M.G.Coy in the line by A & D Sections - B Section in MARTINPUICH. C Section at ACID DROP CAMP. This relief was very successfully carried out without casualties - Except for two Gunners of 143 M.G.Coy 2/Lt. PARBERRY & 2oR A.T.A.	
	3		2/Lt. PARBERRY & 2oR A.T.A. party Cooperated with infantry by assisting them with carrying & thanking for. 1/Sgt Milligan took guns into No mans land dug under that twelve hours & did good work with his guns - Taking on his Enemy Machine Guns during raid 2oR & A.T.A. - C Section relieved B Section in MARTINPUICH	
SHELTER WOOD	3/4		Company relieved by 143 M.G.Coy & returned to SHELTER WOOD CAMP. This was another very good relief and during this tour Coy did a great deal to fill M.T.A. Good had of work was done on Emplacements. Work on Corps line progressed steadily.	
	4/6		No 2446 Sgt Harris awarded D.C.M. for gallant work on 5/6th Nov. Sgt Loam, Sgt Rhodes + SQR to CCS. 2oR & A.T.A.	
	7			
	8			
MARTINPUICH	10		Coy relieved 143 M.G.Coy. B & C Sections in the line. D Section MARTINPUICH	

WAR DIARY
or
INTELLIGENCE SUMMARY

Machine Gun Company.
144th Infantry Brigade.

(Erase heading not required.)

Instructions regarding War Diaries and Intelligence Summaries are contained in F. S. Regs., Part II. and the Staff Manual respectively. Title Pages will be prepared in manuscript.

Place	Date	Hour	Summary of Events and Information	Remarks and references to Appendices
MARTINPUICH	1916 Dec 10		A Section ACID DROP CAMP 10R KOYLI Another good relief.	
	11		Conditions became extremely bad & all work on Reinforcements was another washout. This was owing to lack of labour for the original work & lack of material. Men were just able to do sentry times & keep guns in working order.	
	12		Two guns of 1st & 2nd G. Coy went down at 10.30 pm to support Kept Hand which was threatened with attack or raid.	
	14		1st M.G. Coy. relieved by 4th & 9. G. Coy. C. Section relieved by 48 M.G. Coy.	No P Boy Pk. Hand runner).
	15		B. Section & Section to Reserve MARTIN PUICH relieved by L/Cpl G. Coy. & moved to VILLA CAMP. There was a complicated relief but was very successful.	
			C & D. Sections moved to ALBERT. Early taking on a relief from 4th M.G. Coy.	
Albert.	16		KR & Sections.	for Rest Recreation.
	17		Transport moved to E3. Non Coms & Co/ Cooks. Single strength	
	18		A start was made cleaning guns & equipment. 10R. KOYLI 1 OR for leave	No 35883 Pte Allcorn K.O.Y.L.I.

2449 Wt. W14957/M90 750,000 1/16 J.B.C. & A. Forms/C.2118/12.

WAR DIARY
or
INTELLIGENCE SUMMARY

**Machine Gun Company,
144th Infantry Brigade.**

(Erase heading not required.)

Instructions regarding War Diaries and Intelligence Summaries are contained in F. S. Regs., Part II. and the Staff Manual respectively. Title Pages will be prepared in manuscript.

Place	Date	Hour	Summary of Events and Information	Remarks and references to Appendices
Albert	19		Cleaning was continued. 3 O.R. returned from P.A.	
	20		Cleaning continued. No. 4692 Pte Bell F.C.C.S.	
	21		Company inspected by O.C. Coy. 2 O.R. K P.A. 1 O.R. from P.A. 4660/5 Pte Deal F.C.C.S.	
	22		Belts were oiled + ammunition cleaned. 2 O.R. K P.A. 2 R from P.A.	
	23		Company paraded to get fieldboots ready for Xmas. 5 O.R. for Special leave 2 ships to Pasting K England, auth. G.H.Q. List 614 dated 16/12/15	
	24		Divine Service. 3 O.R. from P.A.	
	25		Xmas day dinner, followed by whist drive + concert	
	26 27		All cleaning was finished. Leave of absence to England. O.C. Coy + 3 O.R.	
	28		Company moved to MILLENCOURT. 1 N.C.O. K P.A. 5762 Pte boyce G. F.C.C.S.	
	29		Visited physical training for efficient and physical drill. Inspection and gymnastic action for efficient machine gunner.	
	30		Company moved to WARLENCOURT. 1 O.R. for leave.	
	31		Divine Service. washing brushes + cleaning guns is mainly of details.	

INTELLIGENCE SUMMARY

**Machine Gun Company,
144th Infantry Brigade.**

(Erase heading not required.)

Summary of Events and Information

Return under review though has not been [so] busy [as] the previous one. The [principal] object in the line has been to [settle] by a better system of relief. Casualties were slight though there was a good deal of sickness. The weather was very bad & so much could be done in any emplacement. The remainder of the month was spent in cleaning guns & in [moves] & gun practices.

For the remainder of the time that the Company is out, it is proposed to direct it into two, one part [entirely] [officers] & to consist of [different] [practice] gunners. The [former] will be given [lectures] range work & [practical] [training] drill, to [enable] all [the] [mechanism] etc until they are [passed] (eyes) as [efficient].

[signature] Lieut for O.C.
Machine Gun Company.
144th Infantry Brigade.

Vol 13

Carpenters
Man Luigi
of Ranchi cucamonga Cuf.
from Oct 16 31st January 1904

Army Form C. 2118.

WAR DIARY
or
INTELLIGENCE SUMMARY

(Erase heading not required.)

Machine Gun Company,
144th Infantry Brigade.

Instructions regarding War Diaries and Intelligence Summaries are contained in F. S. Regs, Part II. and the Staff Manual respectively. Title Pages will be prepared in manuscript.

Place	Date	Hour	Summary of Events and Information	Remarks and references to Appendices
VADENCOURT	1917 Jan 1st		Training	½ Either in RestParade Anthwe on RestParade
	7		Programme of Elementary training in Mechanism. Immediate Action for Reinforcements. Trained Machine Gunners Revise Tactics — opens works — Range finding Picture	
	8		Absorb 30R Reinforcements — 20R to C.E.S. 10R to 69A	
	5			
LIMEUX	8		Company entrained at HEILLY — detrained at Pont REMY — marched to billets at LIMEUX	
	9		TRAINING Further Instruction for Reinforcements in Elementary work was still necessary. Three men who were found to have a very low S.S. of Mechanism in Course of Inspection Elementary firing test. Trained Machine Gunners Open order work. J.D. Range finding on S Ground Posts. Tactical Exercises — Plate Firing — Tactics	
	27			
	No. 28.		Albany Return	
	10			Casualties — Strength decrease Finance
	12.			20R CC.S
	14			20R 9A.
				10R From 9A
	17			
				10R to Base (Munitions) 20R From Base Depot

2449 Wt. W14957/M90 750,000 1/16 J.B.C. & A. Forms/C.2118/12.

WAR DIARY or **INTELLIGENCE SUMMARY**

Army Form C. 2118.
Machine Gun Company,
144th Infantry Brigade.

Place	Date	Hour	Summary of Events and Information	Remarks and references to Appendices
LIMEUX	1916 Jan 25		10R to 7A	Casualties etc.
	26		10R & 7A	
	27		Lt GRAY LWNGT 10R & 8A	
	28		Company entrained at PONT REMY & detrained at CERISY	
CERISY	29		Cleaning of Gun Equipment	
	30		do do	
	31		do do	3oR to 7A

H. F. Hall Capt.
O.C. 144th Machine Gun Company

Vol 14

Confidential

War Diary

of

144 Machine Gun Company

from 1st February 1917 to 28th February 1917.

Volume 14

WAR DIARY or INTELLIGENCE SUMMARY

Army Form C. 2118.

4th Machine Gun Co(y)

Hour, Date, Place	Summary of Events and Information	Remarks and references to Appendices
1917.		Casualties
		FA / CCS / Killed / Wounded / Missing
February		
	1. Company moved from Cerisy to Camp 576 Cappy.	
	2. Company relieved 3 Machine Gun Companies of the 135th Regiment with the Bipette - Barleux line. Relief very satisfactory.	No 37964 Pte Gill myo 626 Pte King 10R 2/Lt Pampling Wounded
Assevré 62 S.N.H.	Dispositions as under:- Right Section:	
Barleux 62 S.W.2	No 2 Gun N.12 676 No 3 Gun O1 c 05 05 No 4 Gun O1 d 1.3. Section H.Q. No 5 Gun O1 c 97 No 6 Gun O1 c 98 No 7 Gun O1 c 69 No 8 Gun (H.Q.) O1 B 60 45 No 9 Gun O1 b 10 75 Support No 10 Gun N6 c 1585 No 11 Gun N66.10.35 No 12 Gun N36 c 72 Reserve 4 Guns at Coy H.Q. N3 S.d 1.1. D Section on Right A Section Left C Section Support B - Reserve	
	3. Reconnoitring of new line.	
	4. Enemy placed heavy barrage on front support + C.T.'s between 11am + 1pm — again (at) further 2pm + 4pm. At 5.30pm an intense barrage was opened on whole front and enemy attempted a series of raids. On Brigade front party attempted to enter trench round No 2 Gun. This Gun was fired throughout barrage by No 21095 Pte Newman. Whole barrage	10R	No 20097 Pte Peckham (Shell shock) No 21088 Pte Annear 12376 Pte Baldwin 22564 Pte Scott

144 Machine Gun Coy.

Army Form C. 2118.

WAR DIARY
or
INTELLIGENCE SUMMARY.
(Erase heading not required.)

Instructions regarding War Diaries and Intelligence Summaries are contained in F.S. Regs., Part II. and the Staff Manual respectively. Title pages will be prepared in manuscript.

Hour, Date, Place	Summary of Events and Information	F.A.	C.C.S.	Killed	Wounded	Missing
1917 February 4	Lifted the team which had been standing to "turned out". No 2223 8 Corp Manns jumped onto parapet by the Gun & seeing Enemy in trench to left of gun position then broke into their midst Bayonetting, forcing them to retire. Remainder of team tried bombing & Engaged Enemy with rifles and Lewis & bombs. He and my party retired the few wounded & Gun inflicted casualties on them. 3 Gunners dead were left in trench & about 20 dead enemy from trenches			No 21088 Pte Chimney died of wounds	No 70613 Pte Engay	
5	Normal	10R 30R				
6/7	A & D Sections relieved by C & B Sections					
8 9	Conditions normal. Work on clearing trenches too. Time not rendered very difficult owing to the very hard nature of the ground.	10R				
	30R from H.Q.					
13th Feb	Company relieved in the line by the 146 M.G. Coy. Returned to Camp at Cappy	10R				
11	Cleaning of Guns, Personal Equipment, Training in Small Box Respirators etc	40R	13th unit 1912 from HQ			
14			No 21046 Pte Clark G 70517 Hancock Q 22624 Billinson 14913 Mabin 6/3/5 Pendlande 21713 Sharevby			
15/19	Company relieved 145 M.G. Cy in the line dispositions the same with following exceptions. Not further cracks & 2 guns holding NPM positions.					
	Thaw started and trenches began to fall in - movement down C.Ts rendered difficult.					

144 Machine Gun Coy

WAR DIARY
or
INTELLIGENCE SUMMARY.
(Erase heading not required.)

Army Form C. 2118.

Hour, Date, Place	Summary of Events and Information	Remarks and references to Appendices
		Casualties
		F.A. / C.C.S. / Killed / Shell Shock & Wounded / Missing
1917 February		
20/21	Machine Gun Coy operated with infantry each doing covering & indirect fire. Reaches Scheme was never about upon aft.	
20/22	C+ D Sections retired. A+ B Sections relief had to be done on the 18th owing to Contd Fire of Ponches 308 Regiments	10R
22-23	7.30 pm Enemy placed heavy barrage on front & Support lines. Machine Guns fired on barrage lines — No apparent machine rinda.	30R
23-24	5.20 am Enemy placed heavy barrage on front & Support lines & attempted to Capture guns at No 2 positions. A Gun deal of close fighting with bomb & others rifle took place. No 35266 Pte Beacom who was sent by Cpl ? to get in touch with post on right did not return. No 21766 Cpl Baker ? did Extremely Good work. M.G's fired on barrage lines. No 5 gun moved to new position No 11 A. ( ) Enemy aeroplane activity, MGs fired on these & secured To hinds them. I promoted Sgt Thwaites & Sargent continued.	No 35266 Pte Beacom / No 21766 Pte Wood I. 10R
25.	145 M G Coy relieved Bde Section in the line then relieving A+D Section who returned to Camp 52 Coppy	

(73969) W.4141—463. 400,000. 9/14. H.&J.Ltd. Forms/C. 2118/10.

144 Machine Gun Coy.

WAR DIARY
or
INTELLIGENCE SUMMARY.

Army Form C. 2118.

(Erase heading not required.)

Place	Date	Hour	Summary of Events and Information	Casualties					Remarks and references to Appendices
				F.A.	C.C.S.	Killed	Wounded	Missing	
	1917 Sep 26		144 M G Coy relieves 13th Coy below & by F.A. who returned to Camps to Coppy.	3 OR					
	27		Cleaning of equipment etc						
	28		do. Working Party of 1 Officer + 80 OR	18 OR	9 OR 1 officer – evacuated	1 OR (accidental)	5 OR	1 OR	
			9 Run Foremanto		Strength increases from PB 4 Reinforcements 12 OR				

A.P. [signature]
Capt. Commanding
144th Machine Gun Company
144th Infantry Brigade

Confidential

War Diary

of

14th Machine Gun Company.

from 1st March 1917 to 31st March 1917

Vol 15

Volume 15

WAR DIARY or INTELLIGENCE SUMMARY

Army Form C. 2118.

Machine Gun Company,
144th Infantry Brigade.

Instructions regarding War Diaries and Intelligence Summaries are contained in F. S. Regs., Part II. and the Staff Manual respectively. Title pages will be prepared in manuscript.

(Erase heading not required.)

Place	Date	Hour	Summary of Events and Information	Casualties					Remarks and references to Appendices
				To FA	From FA	C.C.S.	Killed	Shell Shock & Wounded	
Camp P56 Cappy	1917 March 1		Cleaning of guns & equipment	1	–	–	–	–	Missing
	2			–	–	–	–	–	
	3		Company relieves the 143· M.G. Coy, taking over the Divisional Line. Gun positions in Bouchez Sector – Eight in Lamotte-Etr. Sector. Town in front of Coy H.Q.	2	1	No 57375 Pte Gawthorn	–	No 70796 Pte Wiltshire A No 82304 Pte Ward G.	
	4-5	5·15am	Machine Gun barrage was delivered to assist operations of Corps on left. Thus Aeroplane hostile did not take place. Enemy planes active. One flying low sky dropped a bomb on the A.A. position wounding two men. Enemy aviation & machine gun fire. This reported behind his lines.					No 2797 Pte James. H	
	5-7					No 68519 Pte Dunlop. I.	–	–	
	7		Coy relieved by 143 & 145 M.G. Coys & returned to Camp P.56 Cappy						
	8		Cleaning of guns Equipment bathing &c. A Section was sent up the line on two occasions to assist in M.G. barrage. But this was postponed	1	–	No 58874 Pte Gawdry J.	–	–	
	12								
	13		Coy relieves 145 M.G. Coy in the line.						
	14 15		Conditions normal, except that Enemy appeared very nervous, firing M.G's from every angle and a good deal of the shelling appeared like from single guns. Fine behind picture continues.	4 1	1	No 36551 Pte O'Hanlon. EG.	–	–	
	17	1·30am	A barrage raid was made by the 7th & 8th Bn on La Maisonette Machine Guns placed a heavy barrage on the flanks from two town. This raid was completely successful and practically no enemy rear				1	No 9958 Pte Goltass A	
								No 22562 Lcpl Harvey A	
				18	2	4	1	4	

Army Form C. 2118.

WAR DIARY
or
INTELLIGENCE SUMMARY.

(Erase heading not required.)

Machine Gun Company,
144th Infantry Brigade

Instructions regarding War Diaries and Intelligence Summaries are contained in F.S. Regs., Part II. and the Staff Manual respectively. Title pages will be prepared in manuscript.

Place	Date	Hour	Summary of Events and Information	Casualties				Remarks and references to Appendices
				To F.A. From F.A.	C.C.S.	Killed	Shell Shock & Wounded	
LAMOTIONETTE TRENCHES	1917 March 17		War Diary. During the day the German front line system opposite No Divisional front was occupied & patrols pushed out to the Canal. At mid. No. 879 gun who moved into LAMOTIONETTE meeting heavy M.G. M.T.M. & L.G. fire also met out with heavy M.G. & rifle fire. Gun crew in by enemy shell.	10	4	1	4	Missing 1
	18		No. 617 gun moved to Verma Trench & No. 1 & 2 guns to O.P. behind DANIEL ALLEY. Our outposts continued	2 2	No. 8585 Pte Spencer A. No. 3/955 Pte Dunn H. 47805 Munition			
	20		to make progress & entered PERONNE – etc. Guns withdrawn from LAMOTIONETTE & two guns moved out to the Canal. Guns withdrawn from LAMOTIONETTE & two guns moved out to DOINGT-MESNIL line.	3 1	No. 15710 Pte French F. No. 2187 Pte Brass A.			
CAPPY	21st		144th Inf. Brigade crossed river at PERONNE took over outpost line.	3 1	No. 2101 Pte Leonard S.			
	22 24 25		Company returned to Camp 516 Preparation for advance — Packing of fighting lumber — Getting gear & kit etc. Reinforcements 100 P	2 3	No. 53308 Pte Dutmart G.H.			
			Coy moved into PERONNE	- 1 1 -	No. 31095 Pte Hughes James			
PERONNE	28		Training for advance	-	No. 54741 Pte Barnes W.			
TINCOURT	29		Company moved to TINCOURT & advised 145 M.G.Coy 2 guns in VILLERS FAUCON - 3 guns in Divisional Reserve line.	1	No. 31035 Sgt Genender Pte Sutch Pte Jones A.			
				21 12	14	1	4	

Machine Gun Company,
144th Infantry Brigade.

Army Form C. 2118.

WAR DIARY
or
INTELLIGENCE SUMMARY.
(Erase heading not required.)

Instructions regarding War Diaries and Intelligence Summaries are contained in F. S. Regs., Part II. and the Staff Manual respectively. Title pages will be prepared in manuscript.

Place	Date	Hour	Summary of Events and Information		Casualties			Remarks and references to Appendices
				To F.A. From F.A.	C.C.S.	Killed	Shell Shock & Wounded	
TINCOURT	1917 March 30		Company cooperated with 4th Glos. in attack on St. EMILIE - flanking fire being given from both flanks and covering fire from behind. A Section relieved	21	17 No 82191 Pte Kirby A.	1	4	Shell Shock Missing
	31st		143 M.G. Coy with 2 Guns in SEAUCOURT. 2 Guns moved from VILLERS-FAUCON to ST EMILIE 2 Guns took up positions on high ground to East.	22/2	15	1	4	
			POINTS					
			1. Strength of two officers per section & Transport Officer.					
			2. Increased communication Section required & motor cyclers.					
			3. Establishment inadequate					
			4. Horses required for all officers for advance.					
			Other Tactical & Technical lessons sent in accordance with G.H.Q. N°OB/2007					

[signature]
Capt.
Cmdg. Machine Gun Company,
144th Infantry Brigade.

Confidential

Vol 16

War Diary
of
144; Machine Gun Company.
/48

from 1st April 1917
to 30th April 1917.

Volume 16.

Army Form C. 2118.

**Machine Gun Company,
144th Infantry Brigade.**

Instructions regarding War Diaries and Intelligence
Summaries are contained in F. S. Regs., Part II.
and the Staff Manual respectively. Title pages
will be prepared in manuscript.

WAR DIARY
or
INTELLIGENCE SUMMARY.
(Erase heading not required.)

Place	Date 1917	Hour	Summary of Events and Information	Remarks and references to Appendices
LONGAVESNES	April 1st	5.30am	The Worcester Regt. & 6th Glos. Regt. & Units of 143 Inf. Brigade attacked EPÉHY & PEZIERE. Company co-operated in this attack see Appendix A. A Section being moved up to St. Emilie. B Section being moved up to St. Emilie in the Early morning & were eventually relieved. A Section — having 4 guns in vicinity of EPEHY. 2 guns working on spur East of St Emilie. — 2 guns working on spur F.25 & F.26. A Section returned to Coy H.Q.	
	2nd		Company H.Q. moved to TINCOURT WOOD	
TINCOURT WOOD	3rd		Company relieved by 143rd M.G. Coy & returned to TINCOURT WOOD	
	4th		Cleaning of guns and equipment.	
	5th	5am	143rd Inf. Bde attacked LEMPIRE BASSE BOULOGNE & RONSSOY. 8th Worcester Regt attacked cliffs & spur on right flank — Two guns being taken over from 39th Division & moved back during afternoon. Company co-operated in this attack (See Appendix A). A Section being in Divisional Reserve with 7th Glos Regt.	
	6th		Preparation for move into the line	
VILLERS FAUCON	7th		Company relieves 143rd M.G. Coy dispositions 6 guns in the line 2 support E. St EMILIE. 8 guns with Coy H.Q. Knobcar[?] VILLERS FAUCON.	
	8th		Dispositions reorganised — Chalk bluffs & ridge in F.28.d &c taken over from 59th Division.	

A5834 Wt. W4973/M687 750,000 8/16 D.D. & L. Ltd. Form/C.2118/13.

Army Form C. 2118.

**Machine Gun Company,
144th Infantry Brigade.**

WAR DIARY
or
INTELLIGENCE SUMMARY.
(Erase heading not required.)

Instructions regarding War Diaries and Intelligence Summaries are contained in F. S. Regs., Part II. and the Staff Manual respectively. Title pages will be prepared in manuscript.

Place	Date	Hour	Summary of Events and Information	Remarks and references to Appendices
VILLERS FAUCON	1917 April 9th		2/Lt. G. Pemberton & Sgt. Rustle WOUNDED.	
	10	1am	Cellar in VILLERS FAUCON blown up by explosion of mine — Sgnal section living in this cellar 6 O.R. was killed.	
	11	5am	5th Worcester Regt. attacked xrds in F.29. The company was unable to co-operate — but 1 Gun from Bath. BOULOGNE was laid to assist counter-attack.	
	13th	4am	The Worcester's overnight 4th Bn Regt. on left attacked trench on ridge from F.29.b — F.17.b. Company co-operated. See Appendix A. Company relieved by 145 M.G. Coy & returned ETINCOURT WOOD	
ETINCOURT WOOD	14th		Cleaning of gun equipment — belts etc. personal equipment.	
	16th		Inspection by B.G.C.	
	17th		O.C. Lieut LOWE noted new MARCH xs to K.5. Central at 8am to be in bivouac. Route AT4.3.TM4.37.B34 in their attack on the line GUILLEMONT FARM TOMBOIS FM CATELET COSE & PETIT PRIEL FM	
	18th 19th		2/Lt. MACKAY — 2/Lt. EDMONSON taken on strength. Relieved — 145 M.G. Coy in the line.	

Army Form C. 2118.

Machine Gun Company,
144th Infantry Brigade.

WAR DIARY
or
INTELLIGENCE SUMMARY.
(Erase heading not required.)

Instructions regarding War Diaries and Intelligence Summaries are contained in F. S. Regs., Part II. and the Staff Manual respectively. Title pages will be prepared in manuscript.

Place	Date	Hour	Summary of Events and Information	Remarks and references to Appendices
VILLERS FAUCON	1917 April 20 } 21 } 22 }		Re-sighting of gun positions and setting of anti aircraft. Four guns were kept in Brown Line & four pushed forward to support out post line. Vedettes for our guns kept up on the Knoll Gillemont Fm & Quennemont Fm, valleys and approaches.	
	23.		Preparation for attack on COPSE & Spur A19 & C.E. GILLEMONT Fm. & KNOLL	
	24	3.45 am	Company co-operates with 8th Worcester Regt. 5th R. Bn. Pro. Regt. in attack on above places	See Appendix B
	25	11 pm	Company co-operates with 7th Worcester Regt & 4th Glos. Regt. in renewed attack on above places	
	26 } 27 }		Continuation of attack Company relieved by 145 M.G. Coy.	
	28. 29 30.		Cleaning of guns personal equipment etc. Company relieved 143rd M.G. Coy. Consolidation of positions etc	

Map References 62 @ N.E. 62 z. 13
1/20,000.

[signature]
Capt. O.C. 144th M.G. Coy

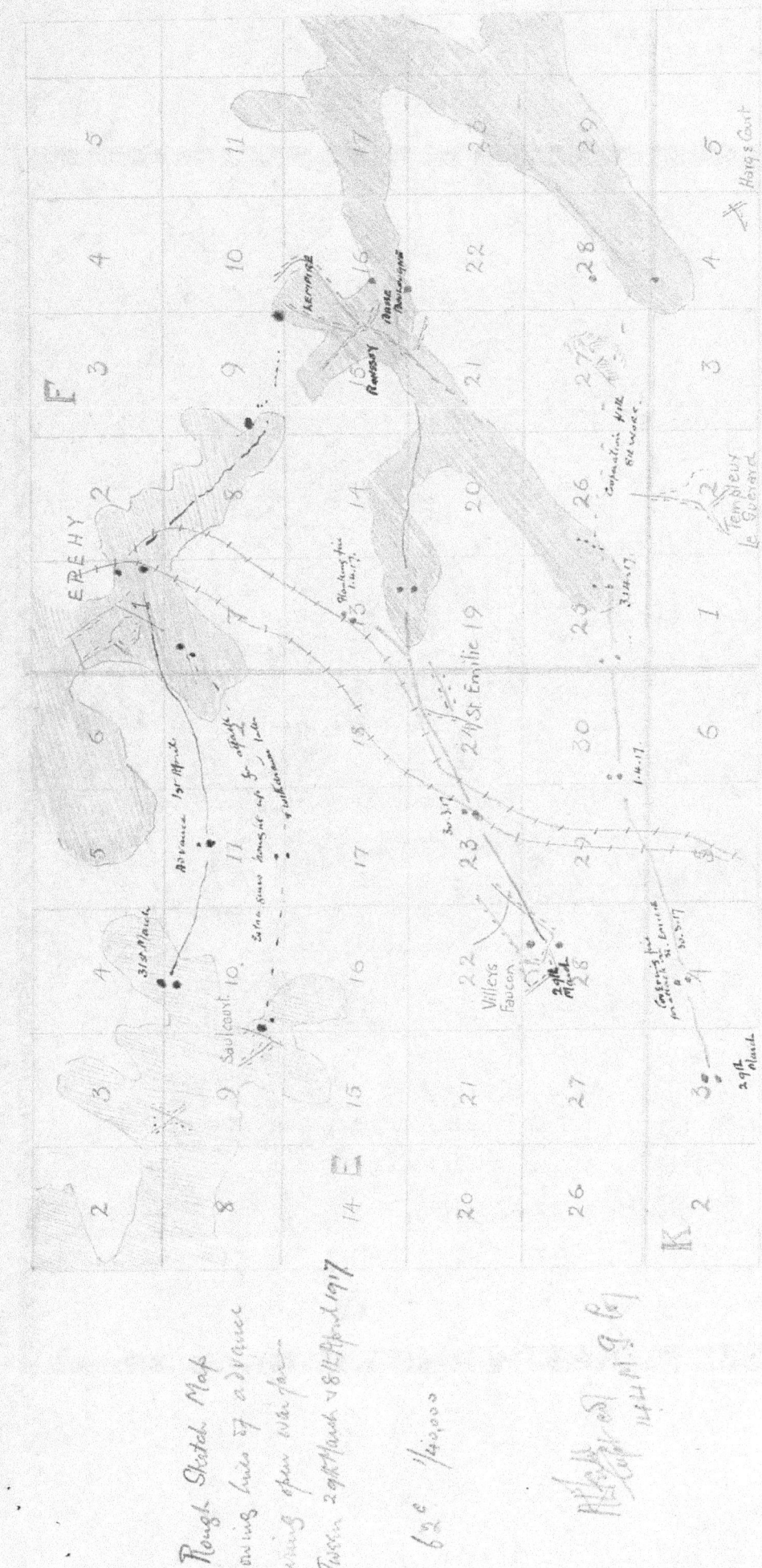

Appendix B.

Operations against:—
Copse + Spur (A19 a + c) — GILLEMONT F<u>m</u>
+ THE KNOLL F6c + F12a
24 + 25th April 1917

3.45 am 24.4.17.

The Company co-operated in attack made by 8th Worcesters on RIGHT + 6th Glos. Reg<u>t</u> on LEFT against Copse + Spur in A19 a + c — GILLEMONT F<u>m</u> + THE KNOLL

Dispositions prior to attack

The Line was held by 8 Guns — Four in BROWN or Support Line (½ A + ½ D) Four Guns in Front System (½ B + ½ C)

Two Guns under 2/Lt Edmondston (B Section) in a position of readiness to support consolidation of GILLEMONT F<u>m</u> — approx objectives A13 b 21 + between A7 d 90 + A7 d 23.

Two Guns under Lt Oakford (C Section) in position of readiness to support consolidation of THE KNOLL — objectives either flank of THE KNOLL

Four guns in Local Support under 2/Lt. HEWSON in F23d (½ D + ½ A)

Coy Command Post F16 a 98 near Bde Command

Post.
Communication   By Relay Runner Posts.

(2) The attacks on the COPSE & KNOLL were unsuccessful. 2/Lt Edmondston moved forward about 4.15am towards GILLEMONT F— with 2 guns, having orders that one of the guns holding the line should move up Sap in F24a and establish itself there to fire down valley towards BONY. On the way to objectives for consolidation 2/Lt Edmondston was asked to bring up both guns to left flank as Bosch were counter attacking there. Both guns moved into position at left objective therefore & were able to force enemy to retire — several extremely good targets with direct observation being obtained at close range. Both guns remained in position on left while officer reconnoitred for right position — having sited this he sent back for gun in Sap head but was unable to get this gun as it had been ordered to go forward by an infantry officer.

As counter attack appeared imminent about 8 am 2/Lt Edmondston withdrew about 100-150y in order to obtain fire both N. & S. Enemy barrage started with enemy following closely behind. Both guns were able to give very useful support to infantry when forced to retire & withdrew to successive positions until reaching original line from which they were able to keep down enemy rifle fire.

Guns under Lt. Oakford did not move forward as attack did not succeed.

11/pm. 24.4.17   Attack was continued
4th Royal Berks (Right) 7th Worcesters
Centre & 4th Gloucesters LEFT.

Dispositions of Company as for morning attack with exception that 3 guns under Lt. Hewson were prepared to assist in consolidation of right objective.
Objectives Given   2 guns either flank of spur
                    1 gun at head of valley.
2 guns under Lt. Edmondston prepared to consolidate GUILLEMONT F^m Objectives Given as for morning attack. 3 guns under Lt. Oakford prepared to assist in consolidation of THE KNOLL. Objectives given as for morning attack with 3rd gun in valley between THE KNOLL & GUILLEMONT F^m

The attack on the RIGHT was unsuccessful

and the position at GILLEMONT F^m was obscure for a long time. In addition the two guns ready to go forward lost officer, Sgt & both team commanders in addition to one of the guns & 4 men. A gun was however got up to Sap-head in F24a.

On the left the position was obscure on the left & left flank but two guns were moved forward by Lt Oakford to positions approx. F18a 7.8 & F12c34. These teams dug in before actual daylight. They were continually visited by Lt Oakford during the day. At dusk an enemy counter attack developed but as infantry withdrew the guns were forced to do so after firing about a belt.

They were however taken forward again

1.5.17

[signature] (Capt)
144 M.G. Coy

Statement of Casualties for month ending 30th April 1917.

Date.	Casualties				
	F.A.	C.C.S.	Killed	Shell Shock Wounded	Missing
April 1.	1	-	No 70595 Pte Diggs		
2.	1	-		E.9 22562 Cpl Maund. W.	
3.	1	-			
4.	1	-			
7.	2	-		3312 Pte Ellis R.	
8.	1	-			
10.	2	-		21016 Pte Arkell R. 2nd Lt Pemberton G.	
				51474 · Carpenter J. 17920 Sgt. Rendle C.	
				22559 · Stevenson H.	
				57848 · Turner A.	
				21099 · McIntosh A.	
				21049 · Essex W.	
12.	-	1			
15.	1	-			
17.	-	2			
18.	1	-		30332 L/Cpl Coleman W.	
20.	-	1		70095 L/Cpl Evans J.	
22.	-	-	70617 Pte Harris H.		
24.	1	-			
25.	2	-		2nd Lt Edmonston J.S.	
				24607 Sgt Steele H.J.	
				22299 Cpl Clements J.	
				9728 Pte Jones E.G.	
				4306 · Cumperness J.	
				55322 · Brown A.	
27.	1	-			
28.	2	-			
29.	2	-			

Confidential

Vol 17

War Diary
of
1st Motor Machine Gun Company

14th May to 31st May 1917
1st May to 31st May 1917

(VOL. XVII)

Army Form C. 2118.

Machine Gun Company, 144th Infantry Brigade.

WAR DIARY or INTELLIGENCE SUMMARY.

(Erase heading not required.)

Ref: 62 c/40000 & 57 c/40000

Place	Date	Hour	Summary of Events and Information	Remarks and references to Appendices
TEMPLEUX	1917 May 1st		Important of employment etc: 125 M.G. By. relieved A. Section left of Brigade line. The Section returning to Villers Faucon after relief. Two new M.G. teams were left with relieving teams until dawn 3rd inst.	
VILLERS FAUCON	2nd		125 M.G. Coy. relieved remainder of Company. D Section Right Front, C Section Right Support and Reserve. Two new M.G. teams remained until dawn on 3rd inst. Company returned to Villers Faucon.	
TINCOURT	4th 5th		Company moved to Tincourt. 2/Lt. H.C.R. Stubbs taken on strength. 2/Lt. E. Diode taken on strength.	
BUIRE	6th		Company moved to camp outside Buire.	
	7th		No. 15530 Cpl Gabriel J. No. 9728 Pte. Jones G.E. courtmartialed. Military neglect. As the Company had been in the line for a considerable time. Inspection of kit etc was most necessary and a large part of the time had to be allotted to Squad & Arms Drill in order to tighten discipline and smarten up the men. Pistols & musketry practice was also carried out, and training of depots in Elementary Gun work	
	9th		in our training elements.	
PERONNE	12th 5pm		Company moved to Peronne.	
COMBLES	13th 5:30am		Company moved to Combles via Clery & Maurepas.	
FREMICOURT	14th 6:20am		Company moved to Fremicourt via Le Transloy & Beaumé. Company relieves 32 M.G.Coy in Beaumetz – Morchies line. (Div: Reserve) Bde lecture going into the line.	

WAR DIARY
Machine Gun Company, 144th Infantry Brigade

(Erase heading not required.)

Place	Date	Hour	Summary of Events and Information	Remarks and references to Appendices
	1917.			
TREMICOURT	May 16th		CAPT A.L. FIELD awarded M.C. N.22524 Sgt Ladler awarded Military Medal.	
	18th		A & D Sections relieved C & B Sections	
MORCHIES	21st		Company relieved 143 M.G. Coy; in LEFT front & support B & C section & ½ A section in the line ½ A section Local Reserve D. Section Reserve. This relief was complicated by having 8 guns in div. line which had to be relieved by 143 M.G. Coy.	
	21st, 28th, 24th, 27th		Reconnoitring of line. This was made difficult, owing to impossibility of movement by day & length of line. Positions were improved and slightly altered. 7 O.R Reinforcements, 2/Lt E. CLODE wounded.	
	29th		Company relieves 143 M.G. Coy in Div line and was relieved by them in LEFT FORWARD SECTOR returns A & B Sections returning to FREMICOURT & the rest.	
	30		Company moved to CHATEAU grounds HAPLINCOURT.	
			The month with a view has been rather eventful. Programme of training has miscued at BOIRE was only started, and there has been little chance of doing more than attempt to keep up a standard of efficiency in Elementary Gun work.	

Walker Capt
144 M.G. Coy.

Army Form C. 2118.

**Machine Gun Company,
144th Infantry Brigade.**

WAR DIARY
or
INTELLIGENCE SUMMARY.
(Erase heading not required.)

Instructions regarding War Diaries and Intelligence Summaries are contained in F. S. Regs., Part II. and the Staff Manual respectively. Title pages will be prepared in manuscript.

Statement of Casualties for month ending 31.5.17

Date	Hour	C.C.S.	Wounded	Killed	Remarks
1916 May	To F.A. / From F.A.				
1	— / —	—	—	—	
2	— / —	1	—	—	
3	— / —	—	—	—	
5	— / —	—	—	—	
6	4 / —	—	—	—	
8	2 / —	—	1	—	
9	— / 3	—	—	—	
10	— / —	1094 Pte Childs A. 5717 " Cullinan A. 15541 " Gibbons E.	—	—	
11	— / —	—	—	—	
12	— / 3	72160 Pte fortnight A. 22546 Cpl Tolley T. 65209 Pte Stoppos A.C.	—	55322 Pte Brown A. died of wounds 30.4.17	
15	— / —	—	—	—	
17	— / —	—	1	—	
20	— / —	—	—	—	
22	— / —	—	—	—	
24	1047 / —	—	—	—	
25	292 / —	—	—	—	
27	— / 1014	—	—	—	2nd Lt E. Clode

Reinforcements received during month:

	Off.	O.R.
1st May	—	—
5th "	1	1
9th "	—	2
18th "	—	1
24th "	—	7
	2	10

Summary.

	To Army From		C.C.S.		Wounded		Killed		Reinforcements	
	Off	O.R.	Off	O.R.	Off	O.R.	Off	O.R.	Off	O.R.
	1	13	1	14	—	7	—	1	2	10

May 31st In F.A. 3 other ranks.

144 Machine Gun Company.

War. Diary.

from. 1st June 1917.   To. 30th June. 1917.

Volume. 18.

"Confidential"

Confidential

Vol 18

War Diary
14th Coy Machine Gun Company
1st June to 30th June 1917.

(Vol. XVIII)

Army Form C. 2118.

WAR DIARY
or
INTELLIGENCE SUMMARY.
(Erase heading not required.)

Machine Gun Company, 143rd Infantry Brigade

Instructions regarding War Diaries and Intelligence Summaries are contained in F. S. Regs., Part II. and the Staff Manual respectively. Title pages will be prepared in manuscript.

Place	Date	Hour	Summary of Events and Information	Remarks and references to Appendices
HAPLIN COURT	1917 Jan 1st		A + B Sections training.	
	2nd		A + B Section relieved C + D Sections in the front line.	
	3rd		C + D Sections inspection and Lewis gun practice under the Brigade Machine Gun Officer	
	4th			
	5th			
MORCHIES	6th		Relieved 143 M.G. Coy. C Section in pos. 1,2,5 & 6 locations (16c.25.80 – D19.c.0.4 – J36.9.55) (12k.90.75, J26.05.90 – D26.c.2.4 – D25b 55.05) D Section at Coy HQ J22.6.7. A Section J10a57 – J9.a.5.0. Platoons at Coy HQ J22.6.7. and B Section in reserve 1911 c 6 1. Coy Field H.Q. Graincourt	
	7th			
	8th		Improvements, slight alteration in position.	
	9th		Enemy new positions were dug to the left section to assist in a Chinese attack by the 20th regt. divisions to take place on the following day. This was subsequently postponed. A section relieved C section who are disposing of TA. B Section relieved D section who returned to reserve Machi. M.P. B Section cooperation with 6th Brigade (on left) during a raid made by him 1300 2ft being fired into small wire in D.14 central. A section independent. Shot 4th G.co. Post during an attempt/flight raid on an enemy/ pt on CAMBRAI Rd K16. Tadpole Copse about 1100 rounds being fired. In TADPOLE COPSE shack in D.24a No. 3 gun moved forward to J.10.6.1.8 equally 1 gun fired down sunken road B + D section fired with 6 gun for the Chinese attack arranged for the 9th arranged from D14a 40 85 K D8c 45 60 the remaining 7 bran used to barrage enemy trench from D14a 20 75 K D14 6 40 65 then lifting to SUPPORT LINE/m D8c 30 17 K D8 d 40 01 then returning on Chinese being lifted terminates between 13-14 thousand rounds were fired to first objective. A + C section being relieved by 143 17.G. Coy C relieving a section of 143 17.G. Coy in the front line (left) A section returning to HAPLIN COURT B + D section left F.P. were relieved by 143 M.G. Coy. D section relieving a section of 143 M.G. Coy in Sect. line (right) B section HQ returning to HAPLIN COURT.	
	14th			
	15th			

Army Form C. 2118.

Machine Gun Company,
144th Infantry Brigade.

WAR DIARY
or
INTELLIGENCE SUMMARY.
(Erase heading not required.)

Instructions regarding War Diaries and Intelligence Summaries are contained in F. S. Regs., Part II. and the Staff Manual respectively. Title pages will be prepared in manuscript.

Place	Date	Hour	Summary of Events and Information	Remarks and references to Appendices
HAPLINCOURT	16th to 18th		Both Infantry training for A & B Sections. A & B section relieved C & D in Brit. line.	
	19th 20th 21st		Both Infantry training for C & D section.	
	22nd		Relieved 143 M.G. Coy. C section on the right in but 1.2.5 & 6 positions. D section on the left in Nos. 7,8,9,10 positions. A section having 2 guns at 3 & 9 positions and 2 guns at Coy H.Q. B section in reserve. No 8 position moved from J.10 a 5.7 to J.10 f 1.8.	
	23rd		Improvement of Positions. Making Shelter dugouts. Enemy trenches & roads were searched during the night with indirect fire.	
	24th 25th 26th		to B section relieved D section in Nos. 7,8,9,10 positions. A section relieved C section who went into reserve. D section having 2 guns at Coy. H.Q. & 2 guns in Nos. 3 & 4 positions.	
	27th		No.10 gun moved from Shells the position D. North (new) improved. 1st Neilson acting O.C. D.K.S.A. M.G. Coy. 2nd Division came up to the line before taking it over from us.	
	28th 29th		144 M.G. Coy relieved by the 8th M.G. Coy. This relief was carried out the day before the Infantry relieved the battalion relief; though the weather made the trenches difficult for the Guides. 2 men were left to cool gun position for 24 hours.	
	30th		Very little of importance has occurred during the month; the line has been very quiet and our casualties have been few. Owing to the fact that we have had 8 guns in the Divisional line (MORCHIES - BEAUMETZ) when the Company has been out there has been little facility for doing any training. The health of the men has been quite good.	

A 8534 Wt W4973/M657 750000 8/16 D.D.&L.Ltd. Form C.2118/13

Arthur D Vincent Capt.
Commanding 144th Inf Bde M.G. Coy.

144 Machine Gun Company

Statement of Casualties etc.   June 1917

Date	To F.A.	From F.A.	C.C.S.	Wounded	Transfers
1917 June 4	–	–			
5	1	1	15335 A/Cpl Dixon 64838 Pte Jackson P. 72413 Pte Potter.		
6	1	1	S. Shaw		
9	1	1			
10	1	12	82305 Pte Ruddle F.		
12	–	–			
14			22550 4/Cpl Dancey W. 65341 Pte West T.		
18					
24	–	1			15376 Pte Lumb E R. to Base. under age.
27	1	–	63716 Pte Butcher V.		
29	–	18/5 (2/Lt R.G. Foskey from C.C.S)		1	2.
	3 1 – 4		6		

Reinforcements received during month.

	Off.	O.R.
June 1st	2	–
4	–	1
9	1	2
12	1	2
21	1	–
29	1	2
	3	11

Transfers.

Capt. A.L. Feild to Grantham.

15376 Pte Lumb E R. to Base. under age.

Summary.

	To F.A		From F.A		C.C.S.		Wounded		Transfers		Reinforce.	
	Off	OR	Off	OR	Off	OR	Off	OR	Off	OR	Off	OR
	1	3	1	4	–	6	–	1	1	1	3	11

June 30th. Strength: 12 Off. _ 177 Other ranks.

Away from Unit   F.A.   1 OR.
                   Leave.   5. OR.
                   Command. M.G 1.
                   Sigs   1.
                   Cookery 1.

No 19

War Diary

144 Machine Gun Company

from 1st July 1917 to 31st July 1917

Volume 19

Army Form C. 2118.

WAR DIARY or INTELLIGENCE SUMMARY.

(Erase heading not required.)

Machine Gun Company, 144th Infantry Brigade.

Instructions regarding War Diaries and Intelligence Summaries are contained in F. S. Regs., Part II. and the Staff Manual respectively. Title pages will be prepared in manuscript.

Place	Date	Hour	Summary of Events and Information	Remarks and references to Appendices
HAPLINCOURT ACHIET-LE-PETIT	July 1st		The Company marched to ACHIET-LE-PETIT. Cleaning of guns & equipment.	
	" 2nd	2 P.M.	The Company moved to BLAIREVILLE below the training area of the Brigade was situated.	
BLAIREVILLE	" 4th " 7th		Training was commenced at & a good deal of infantry training was included the remainder of the time being devoted to exercises in & machine gun work, Visibility & rifle practice.	
Do.	" 8th	4.30 P.M.	Company started by to horse at that notice. It has been for battalions of the brigade were attached this as carrying parts, Preparations for entraining.	
	9th		The Company paraded and marched to BEAUMETZ where they entrained for ST. OMER. The company including transport left under Lieut. Ketcham and left at about 9 P.M.	
ST. OMER	10th	6 A.M.	Company detrained at ST. OMER. Company moved to the training area being attached to the 116 Brigade 39th Division at HOUCE where they held a camp in the vicinity of the village.	
	11th " 15th " 16th	9 A.M.	Training was recommenced. Special attention being paid to barrage firing, anti-aircraft firing Night advance of Company and squad drill were also included. When no special work was in progress to opportunity was given to participating in that work [illegible] & mens. Wells were put thoroughly. The Standard was given some [illegible] practising in hostile guns finding behind a village etc.	
	17th " 20th		Sunday: Training was continued. The Company was [illegible] attached to the 118 Brigade.	
	25th	12.45 P.M.	Orders were received that on stated conditions rifles on the 25th the transport would be dispatched with 117 Brigade and Company permitted & entrain & move & camp in A.30 central (Map Belgium Sheet 28 N.W. 1/20000) Embarking	
		11.30 P.M.	has completed at about 4 P.M. Transport deterred on the POPERINGHE - PROVEN Road, where they were met by advance party under 2/Lt. J. Miller. The transport arrived at their camping ground about 11.30 P.M. having spent the night 2 Lt. J. H. at WORMHOUDT.	
A.29 C.32.52. (Map Belgium Sheet 28NW 1/20000)	22nd	3.30 A.M.	After a march of about 5 miles the Company arrived at its camping ground A.29 C.32.52 (Map Belgium Sheet 26 N.W. 1/20000). Remainder of the day was allotted to rest, improving the camp & cleaning up.	
	23rd 24th		All guns filled etc. kept thoroughly inspected & inspected for sufficient supply of Bombs. Enemy used long bag in cases of little skilling. Rain delayed settling in to in the vicinity.	
	25th		Bangs barring guns. Officers reconnoitered roads to Canal Bank [illegible] BANK. Lts. A.G. Hearne, R.G. Foster also reconnoitered [illegible] positions. Zero day [illegible] mail for 3 days.	
	26th		Remainder of Co entrained to pulverise [illegible] for 2 days. [illegible] outpost at ON.G.O. 39 K. Bgd & determined M.G. officers who were responsible for digging the positions & getting up the ammunition.	

WAR DIARY OR INTELLIGENCE SUMMARY

Army Form C. 2118.

Machine Gun Company, 144th Infantry Brigade.

Instructions regarding War Diaries and Intelligence Summaries are contained in F. S. Regs., Part II. and the Staff Manual respectively. Title pages will be prepared in manuscript.

(Erase heading not required.)

Place	Date	Hour	Summary of Events and Information	Remarks and references to Appendices
A29c 23.52	July 27th		Reconnoitring continued. Whilst reconnoitring on the evening 27th CANAL BANK 2/Lt R.F. Foster and 3 slightly wounded and Sgt. Ahn Keen No 28555 was mortally wounded, and Though strong search was made failed to be found. Parties set out Advance Party 2/Lt. Battle E.B. gun section to CANAL BANK. No ammunition was got up to CANAL BANK, but owing to a heavy + sudden enemy barrage 4 guns & H.E. shells it was impossible to get them to positions.	
	28th		A wiring party. That is [illegible] to the Company engaged in barrage scheme conducted at CANAL BANK. For the barrage the Company was as follows: A battery under 2/Lt Henson (2/Lt Poster being wounded) consists of A Section under 2/Lt Battle + B Section under Lt Boron; B battery under Lt Haines consisting of C Section under 2/Lt Stevens and D Section under 2/Lt Hitkin. A total of 16 guns been about E21d31 and B being about C27b3.9. All the ammunition was got up to the positions that night.	
	29th			
	30th	9 P.M.	Company remained at CANAL BANK during the day, having for their positions about Lt Haines [2nd] at Batallion Hqrs (1st Sussex) Askuchi was consulted at ANZAC TOP FARM.	
			Capt Hellatt (143 M.G. Coy) observed the groups commanders at work.	
	31st	3:50AM	2/Lt Henson the Stoy Battery Commander was counted to B.M.G., Neuve by Here. Zero hour, fire was opened; were continued till Zero + 83 for times left at Zero + 2 two + 8 home 3 minutes the Company retired (CANAL BANK and them to the camp. Though the positions came to fire against dead of building but tyre + after zero reached its casualties.	
			During the month serious reviews the company has been resting + having further instruction how to improve. A large amount of Stuff has but & beginning to happen work as it was the first time to Company had held to innurable attack life was set After all the Calculates etc had been worked out; Previous there performance was extremely registed and glory to the actual schemes. This proved Satisfactory. There was no hostile patrols of great assistance in trolling for ordering during patrols, should be of great assistance in trolling for objects.	

10th Durant Capt.
Att. MG Coy

Appendix A.

(1) The guns in each battery were placed 10 yards apart. The space between the batteries being about

Battery	Location	Firing from 2 no. t to 6 2 no. t		Target	Rate of fire per gun	
A	C 27 d 39	0	10	C17 d 0.2 — C17 c 36	3000 rounds per hour	
		11	18	C17 d 3.5 — C17 c 6.6	3000	Do
		19	1.15	C17 d 7.8 — C17 a 9.1	3000	Do
		1.16	1.23	C17 d 9.2 — C17 c 3.3	3000	Do
B	C 21 d 3.1	0	10	C17 c 36 — C16 b 6.05	2000 rounds per hour	
		11	18	C17 c 6.6 — C16 b 9.2	3000	Do
		19	1.15	C17 a 9.1 — C17 a 2.5	3000	Do
		1.16	1.23	C17 b 3.5 — C17 a 6.9	3000	Do

N.B. Between 70000 & 80000 rounds were fired.

(2) Little trouble was experienced with stoppages, all the barrels were new but there were no surplus ones issued here.

N. Durrat Capt.
144 M.G. Coy

Statement of Casualties etc. July 1917

Date	F. Ambulance		C.C.S Wounded		
	To	From			
1917 July 3	1	-			
4	1	-			
7	3	-			
8	-	1			
12	-	-			
16	1	-	No. 90076 Pte Marshall L.		
17	10	1	No. 22556 L/Cpl Dancey W.D.		
19	1	1			
22	-	1	No. 70601 Pte Binder. C.		
23	3	1	No. 55444 " Cook. P.		
24	1	1	No. 54758 " Brailsford A.	2nd Lieut R.G. Foster	
				No. 22555 Sgt Keen. A.M.	
25	3	-			
29	2	1			
	14	4	5	10ff 1 O.R.	

Reinforcements

1917		
July 5th		from C.C.S.
7		" 220th M.G.Coy
8		from Battalions within Brigade attached for Operations
17		"
22		from Base Depot

	Off	OR
	1	-
	-	-
	1	64
	1	1
	1	1
	-	-
		68

To F.A. / From F.A. / C.C.S. Wounded

To F.A.		From F.A.		C.C.S		Wounded	
Off	OR	Off	OR	Off	OR	Off	OR
1	14	-	4	-	5		

July 31st Strength
After attack

Off 13 / 1 / 14 OR 174 / 66 / 240

Absorbed from Unit
F.A.   Off 1 OR 8
Leave   5
XVIII Corps M.G. Sch. 3
                Off 3 / 17

Vol 20

War Diary.
of
144 M.G. Coy
from 1st August 1917 to 31st August 1917

Volume 20

Confidential

Army Form C. 2118.

Machine Gun Company,
144th Infantry Brigade.

Instructions regarding War Diaries and Intelligence
Summaries are contained in F. S. Regs., Part II.
and the Staff Manual respectively. Title pages
will be prepared in manuscript.

WAR DIARY
or
INTELLIGENCE SUMMARY.
(Erase heading not required.)

Place	Date	Hour	Summary of Events and Information	Remarks and references to Appendices
A39 32 5 2	1 Aug 1917		Training recommenced attention being paid to loss rushes for shell & training the attached men in machine gun work. 2/Lt NEO under Lt BETTS. BROWN, OAKFORD & 2/Lt BETTS HEWSON were sent up to reconnoitre the line between three dates	
	2			
	3			
	4			
	5		A section under Lt Betts relieved 6 guns of the 117th and 228 MG Companies	
DAMBRE CAMP	6	9.30 am	The Coy less A Section moved to Dambre Camp.	
	7		2/Lt Bilefs to Corps rest station with shell shock. 2/Lt Stevens went to take his place. Pte Morton wounded.	
	8		B Section under Lt Brown relieved A section in the line. Pte Forfa missing	
	9		14 men of B section passed A/Cpl Strandridge wounded. Another gun shell C section under Lt OAKFORD relieved B section	
	10		in the line	
	11		training continued with the resting Coys.	
	12		Pte Budge previously reported missing now reported wounded	
	13	3 am	D section relieved C section in the line	
	14		Section cleaning guns ready for the attack on the 16th	
	15		The Coy moved up to Bucket positions. 2/Lt Stevens with 2 guns from B section went up to Morley positions.	
			D Section then marched up to find the Coy at their battle positions. The Coy was divided into 2 batteries of 4 guns	
			C Battery consisting of A section under 2/Lt MACKAY & B section under Lt BROWN. Battery commanded Lt BROWN	
			D Battery consisting of C section under Lt OAKFORD & D section under 2/Lt MILLER. Battery commanded 2/Lt HEWSON.	
	16		C Battery took up position under arrangements made by Lt Browne for barrage work	
			D Battery went forward after the infantry & took up positions about 150 yds the other side of the Steenbeck.	
			Our flat in front of our old front line. D Battery were in position by about 1.15 & opened fire on	
			barrage lines at Zut & H4 Somerville.	
			C Battery were unable to put across to actually coming front on to the guns.	

Army Form C. 2118.

Machine Gun Company,
144th Infantry Brigade.

Instructions regarding War Diaries and Intelligence Summaries are contained in F. S. Regs., Part II. and the Staff Manual respectively. Title pages will be prepared in manuscript.

WAR DIARY
or
INTELLIGENCE SUMMARY.
(Erase heading not required.)

Place	Date	Hour	Summary of Events and Information	Remarks and references to Appendices
	17		C Battery & D Battery remained in position during this day with the guns stood out on temporary lines in case of SOS signal and withdrew at night to Reigersvlei camp	
	18		B section relieved 1 section of the 145 Coy at dawn	
	19		2 guns from B section under 2/Lt PATTERSON went over the Steenbeck in support of an attack made by the 6 Warr	
	20		D section under 2/Lt MILLER relieved B section at dawn. B section returned to Reigersburg camp after relief	
	21		C section under Lt OAKFORD relieved A section in the BUND. A section returned to Reigersburg camp after relief. 2 guns were ordered to support the attack by the 6/Glos on the 22nd. 2 guns from D section were detailed for this.	
	22		The 2 guns from D section went forward & took up position in a newly established MG through the loop holes.	
	23		B section relieved D section	
	24		A section relieved B section. B section relieved C section in the BUND. C section returned to Reigersburg camp after relief	
	25		40,000 rounds of SAA were carried up to the BUND in preparation for the attack. 5 guns to be at ALBERTA at zero. 5 guns to be at HILTON at ". 6 guns in newly assembly trenches zero + 10 minutes. 5 guns at Hilton. 2 guns at Alberta.	
	26		Orders for the attack received from brigade	

WAR DIARY or INTELLIGENCE SUMMARY

Machine Gun Company, 144th Infantry Brigade.

Army Form C. 2118.

(Erase heading not required.)

Instructions regarding War Diaries and Intelligence Summaries are contained in F. S. Regs., Part II. and the Staff Manual respectively. Title pages will be prepared in manuscript.

Place	Date	Hour	Summary of Events and Information	Remarks and references to Appendices
	26 Sept		8 guns in front line as soon as objective is captured	
			2 guns in Hebron	
			6 guns in present front line	
			A & B sections under Lt. Brown were detached to reinforcement & take up position in assembly trenches from Hebron	
			C + 2 teams of D section under 2/Lt Stevens	
	27	1.55	Prompt at zero A & B moved off & took up position without casualties, getting in position just in time to except enemy barrage. C & 2 teams of D adv[anced] also arrived in position without casualties. Nothing definite could be obtained as to how the attack went. A & B sections remained in their position. At 11 p.m. orders were received from Brigade to withdraw 8 guns to Dambre Camp & to have 2 guns at Hebron + 6 in our old front line. A & B section were withdrawn & C section & 2 teams of D were sent to Hebron front line. The 2 teams of D who remained at Hebron were sent to Hebron. The guns kept in the line were relieved by section of the 206 M.G. Coy. The guns after being relieved returned to Dambre Camp.	
	28			
	29	10.30	The Coy proceeded to Poperinghe by train. From thence marched to School camp near Houtkerque Belgium.	
	30			
	31		Reorganising the Coy & starting training attention being paid to squad drill, physical training	

Statement of Casualties   August, 1917.

Date.	F.A To.	F.A from.	C.C.S. Wounded	Killed
1917 August 2	Offr - OR -	Offr - OR -	83068 Pte Ferguson A.	
4	- 1	- 1		
6	- 2	- 1		
7	- 1	- 1		
11	- 1	- 1		
12	- 1	- 1		
14	- 1	- 2	21056 Sgt Constance. H	
			37951 Pte Grogan. J	
			65313 " Sparks. J	
15	- 1	- 1		
16	- 1	- 1		
17	- 1	- 1		
18	- 1	- 1		
19	- 1	- 1		
20	- 1	- 1		
21	- 1	- 1	10944 Pte Childs L	
22	- -	- 1	27299 Cpl Clements. J	See list Attached
			263109 Pte Gray W	
			9370 " Lee S	
23	- 1	- -	57564 " Biddick A.	
24	1	1		
26	- 1	- 1		
30	- 2	- 1		
31	- -	- 1		
	4 15	- 6	9	1 Offr 14 3

Reinforcements.

1917.		
August 14	From C.C.S.	Offr - OR 1
" 15	From Base Depot	- 2
" 17	" " "	- 11
" 21	" " "	- 1
" 22	" " "	- 5
" 26	" " "	- 24
" 27	" " "	- 2
" 29	" " "	- 1
" 30	" " "	Tpt - 12
" 31	" " "	- 5
		1 . 64

	To. F.A	From F.A	C.C.S.	Wounded	Killed	Died of Wounds	Missing
	Offr OR	Offr OR	Offr OR	Offr OR	Offr OR	Offr OR	Offr OR
	4 15	- 6	- 9	1 45	- 14	- 3	- 1

August 31. Strength Offr OR
Attached 11   191
In F.A   1   44
Leave   4   5
Courses   1   8
                 4

Confidential

Vol 21

War Diary

of

144 Machine Gun Company

from 1st September 1917 to 30th September 1917.

Volume 21

Army Form C. 2118.

**Machine Gun Company,
144th Infantry Brigade.**

WAR DIARY
or
INTELLIGENCE SUMMARY.
(Erase heading not required.)

Instructions regarding War Diaries and Intelligence Summaries are contained in F. S. Regs., Part II. and the Staff Manual respectively. Title pages will be prepared in manuscript.

Place	Date	Hour	Summary of Events and Information	Remarks and references to Appendices
SCHOOL CAMP	1917 Sept 1st		Re-organising - re-equipping etc:	
JAN-TER-DIEZEN	17th		Training. Time allotted to :— Infantry work (Arms Drill Squad Drill Company drill) Fire Orders. Indication Recognition of targets. Action of & formations adopted by Concealed & Firing Guns. Barrage Drill.	
	18th		Company entrained ABEELE & detrained AUDRUICQ moving into billets BERTHEN	
BERTIE HEM	19th		Training. Brigade & Divisional Schemes. (Importance & difficulty of Communication & Control - Ammunition Supply) Field Firing (The necessity of perfect fire control brought out, also necessity of practice on 30" range - which is often neglected) Revolver Practice - Rough Ground Drill - Usual inspections & Gas Drill etc.	
	30th			

M.M. Aukett Lieut for O.C.,
Machine Gun Company,
144th Infantry Brigade.

Army Form C. 2118.

**Machine Gun Company,
144th Infantry Brigade.**

WAR DIARY
or
INTELLIGENCE SUMMARY.

(Erase heading not required.)

Instructions regarding War Diaries and Intelligence Summaries are contained in F. S. Regs., Part II. and the Staff Manual respectively. Title pages will be prepared in manuscript.

Place	Date	Hour	Summary of Events and Information	Remarks and references to Appendices
	1917			
	September		Statement of Casualties	
				O/R
C.C.S.	1		58400 Pte Dicken J.	2
	2		8838 " Spencer A.	2
	3			1
	4		Captain Y. M. Dorakt	3
	5		Lieut A.B. Haime	
	6		2/Lieut J.T. Hewson	1
			" N.E. Betts	
	7		36059 Pte Ball C.W.H.	2
	8		No. 22300 Sandy G.W.	2
	9		33317 Erington C.E.	
	11			
	24		9 men transported to 143 M.G.Coy in accordance with instructions from C.M.G.O.	
	26		63237 Pte Cahell. to C.C.S.	
			12158 " Clements S. "	
			33104 " Howlett "	
			4 O/R . 17.	15

(A7091). Wt. W12839/M1293. 75,000. 1/17. D. D. & L., Ltd. Forms/C2118/14.

VM 22

Army Form C. 2118.

WAR DIARY
or
INTELLIGENCE SUMMARY.

(Erase heading not required.)

Machine Gun Company.
144th Infantry Brigade.

Instructions regarding War Diaries and Intelligence Summaries are contained in F. S. Regs., Part II. and the Staff Manual respectively. Title pages will be prepared in manuscript.

Place	Date	Hour	Summary of Events and Information	Remarks and references to Appendices
	1917 Oct.			
BERTHEN	1st		Company entrained AUDRUICQ & detrained at POZELHOEK - marching to BRAKE CAMP	A 30 Central
BRAKE CAMP	2nd		Company parties under 2nd/Lieut MULLER preparatory to infour barrage	
	3rd		Company moved after "tea" to position for barrage	
LINE & REIGERSBURG	4th.		Company fired barrage to assist attack of 143 Inf Bde & moved back at 4pm to REIGERSBERG CAMP	Report on operations
REIGERSBURG CAMP	5th 7th.		This spent in acting the men - cleaning gun equipment & reconnaissance.	4th - 9th October attacks
Line	8th.		Company moved into the line	
	9th.		" co-operated with Brigade in attack	
	10th		Reorganisation consolidation of line. Company relieved by 26 M.G. Coy, and moved to SIEGE CAMP	
SIEGE CAMP	11th			
SCHOOL CAMP	12th		Company moved to SCHOOL CAMP (POPERINGHE)	
	13th		Company entrained at HOPOUTRE for 1st Army area & arrived	
SAVY	14th		SAVY	
VILLERS-AU-BOIS	15th		Company moved to VILLERS-AU-BOIS	
LINE	16th		Company relieved 5th CANADIAN M.G. Coy, in CHAUDIERE SECTOR	

Machine Gun Company.
144th Infantry Brigade.

Army Form C. 2118.

WAR DIARY
or
INTELLIGENCE SUMMARY.
(Erase heading not required.)

Instructions regarding War Diaries and Intelligence Summaries are contained in F. S. Regs., Part II. and the Staff Manual respectively. Title pages will be prepared in manuscript.

Place	Date	Hour	Summary of Events and Information	Remarks and references to Appendices
CHAUDIERE SECTOR	1917 Oct. 16		Dispositions as per attached map. Only 10 guns are taken over owing to 6 having been	
	17		destroyed by shell fire during operations of 9/10 Oct 1917.	
			144 Inf Bde. relieved by Canadian Inf Bde in CHAUDIERE Sector	
	22nd		Gun at T7b25,15 & T7b95,05 withdrawn	
	23rd		Section moved to the vicinity of ZOLLERN HOUSE - Section Transport Lines (AUX RIETZ) Apx B.S. 51/3 NW	
			2 Sections v Coy H.Q. in R.E. huts	
	24		Work started on 2 Emplacements Tg d 9.3. approx.	
	25th		A.C. Sections relieved B.D Sections in the line.	
	26		Work continued on new Emplacements & the improvement of existing Emplacements (switching	
			improvement of forms & field of fire)	
	31st		Keane nights fairly heavy shelling nothing of 27th inst	

[signature] Capt.
Cmdg. Machine Gun Company,
144th Infantry Brigade.

Machine Gun Company,
144th Infantry Brigade.

Army Form C. 2118.

WAR DIARY
or
INTELLIGENCE SUMMARY.
(Erase heading not required.)

Instructions regarding War Diaries and Intelligence Summaries are contained in F. S. Regs., Part II. and the Staff Manual respectively. Title pages will be prepared in manuscript.

Place	Date	Hour	Summary of Events and Information	Remarks and references to Appendices
F.A.	1917 October 2	from 8/10 to 8/10	Statement of Casualties October 1917	
			C.C.S. **Wounded** **Killed**	October 1917
	2		4272 Pte Roe. M. 67445 Pte Ritchard. C. 46902 Pte Harmer. T.	Off OR
	4		64439 " Howe. H. 64477 " Taylor. J. 97769 " Long. C.W.	— 3
	5		7114 " Brooks. C.	— 1
	6		103634 " Cunnington. F	
	7		2058 Sgt Constance. H lt/gnr Pte Morris	— 15
	8		9994 Pte Dutton. J 70412 Pte Potter. J	— 1
	9	at { 60468 " Connolly. J.G 56997 " Dangerfield. R	
		{ 3624 " Osborne. W 14537 " Hopwood. M.	
		{ 82191 " Kilby. M 31156 " Pitchford. G.H	
		{ 109345 " Hall. G	
	10	2	21920 A/Cpl Sykes. J	
	11	1		
	12			
	13	1	81214 Pte Lynagh. J	
	14	2	70613 " Gregory. C.H	
	18			
	19	1	19464 " Scott. E.	
	20	1		
	21	2	47754 " Farlow. R.	
	22	1	Brantham	
	23	1	90075 Pte Fisher. J	
	27	1	103630 " Amos. F	
	29			
		15 — 9	9 10 1 — 7	1 — 23

October 1917
Reinforcements from Base Depot   03
" C.C.S (wounded)   21
" Base Depot (wounded)   28

[signature] Capt.
Cmdg Machine Gun Company,
144th Infantry Brigade.

Dispositions

Prior to relief by
148. M.G. Coy. 1-11-17.

Dispositions.

As taken over from
5th Canadian M.G. Coy.
16.10.17.

23.7

Confidential

War Diary

Vol 23

of

1/8th Bn "Worcestershire Regt.

Feby 1st to Feby 28th 1917

(Vol XXIII)

Army Form C. 2118.

Machine Gun Company
11th Infantry Brigade

INTELLIGENCE SUMMARY.

(Erase heading not required.)

Place	Date	Hour	Summary of Events and Information	Remarks and references to Appendices
BIENVILLER	1916 Feb 29.		low establishment, and owing to the shortage in personnel carrying parties for reliefs have been impossible. This has led to the necessity of relieving only Gun & Spare part box - remainder of Gun Equipment being handed over as Trench Stores — a proceeding which greatly militates against section returns on condition of Gun Equipment and also to the unavoidable misplacement of parts of Gun Equipment. The company transport is very little less than that of a Battalion. A recent Brigade Order enforces that the personnel of all Battalion transports be maintained at 50. The Company Transport has to be run with a personnel of 25 or under.	

H. Fach
Lieut.

144th Brigade.

48th Division.

1/7th BATTALION

WORCESTERSHIRE REGIMENT

FEBRUARY 1916

144th Brigade.

48th Division.

1/7th BATTALION

WORCESTERSHIRE REGIMENT

MARCH 1 9 1 6

144th Brigade.

48th Division.

1/7th BATTALION

WORCESTERSHIRE REGIMENT

APRIL 1916

144th Brigade.
48th Division

1/7th BATTALION

WORCESTERSHIRE REGIMENT

M A Y 1 9 1 6

144th Brigade.
48th Division.

1/7th BATTALION

WORCESTERSHIRE REGIMENT

JUNE 1916

Appendices attached:- Schemes for raids.

Raid on German Trenches night 15th/16th June 1916 by 7th Battalion
The Worcestershire Regiment.

SCHEME FOR RAIDING GERMAN TRENCHES.

GENERAL IDEA.
Infantry.

The General Idea was to raid the German trenches at point K.17.d.15.25. with two assaulting parties, one to work to the right and one to work to the left, and a covering party, the Sappers to blow up wire with Bangalore Torpedoes. The point of exit selected was the 1st.Barricade on the SERRE Road K.17.c5.1. and the point of entering the trenches again between the 1st and 2nd.Barricades.

Artillery.

It was arranged that the Artillery should form a barrage on the front line German trenches on the left and the right of the selected portion of trenches to be raided using Shrapnel and on the 2nd.line in rear of the selected portion of trench using Percussion H.E. It was also arranged that in case of emergency a barrage might be brought to bear in front of the left or right flank.
Also the right flank was covered by Machine Gun fire if required, and the signal for them to open fire arranged.

Detail.

The composition of each of the assaulting parties was as folows in the following order:-
1 Officer and 8 other ranks consisting of:-
2 Bayonet men, armed with rifle and bayonet and bombs.
2 Bombers, armed with bombs and bludgeons.
Their duties were to bomb along the trench and block the trench if a dug-out was encountered.
1.Officer   armed with revolver and bludgeon.
4.Other men   armed with Bombs, revolvers, one rifle and bayonet also provided with electric torches and lengths of rope.
Their duties were to deal with the contents of any dug-outs encountered.
Each assaultingparty carried one ladder.

Tape laying party.
1.N.C.O. & 4 men, armed with rifles and bayonets and bombs and provided with reel of tape.

Sappers Party.
1.N.C.O. & 5 sappers, armed with Bayonets and bombs and 8 14 foot bangalore Torpedoes.

Covering party.
2 Officers & 15 other ranks including 2 Signallers, 1 Stretcher Bearer Lewis Gun and team on the left flank.
O.C., 2 Signallers, Artillery F.O.O. & Signaller, between the 1st and 2nd Barricades.

Orders.
Orders issued the covering party were to get into position first and when this was accomplished a message to that effect would be sent over the telephone to O.C.
The remainder would be sent out in their proper order and when they were in position the message "open fire" would be sent to O.C.
This was the signal arranged with the Artillery to commence fire (Sections fire 30 seconds)
The party detailed for laying the tape would then run out the tape from the covering party to the point in the German wire to be dealt with, when this was completed a report would be made to O.C. covering party who would send a messeage by telephone to O.C. "ready to begin" this message would be passed to the Artillery and was the prearranged signal with the Artillery to quicken fire

Scheme for raid on trenches contd.

to Section fire 20 seconds.   and to withdraw the Sappers.
The sappers party would then move along the tape to the German wire and commence operations. When the wire was blown up a report would be made th Officers Commanding Assaulting parties and covering party.
O.C. covering party would then report to O.C. O.K. (wire is cut)
The assaulting parties would then move forward into the German trench Officers Commanding assaulting parties had arranged signals for withdrawing their parties from the German trench. These parties would then move back down the tape via the covering party (where they would be checked) to the point selected for re-entering the trench and when this was accomplished covering party would be withdrawn, arrangements having been made to check them as they entered our trench.
In the event of the sappers not being able to get through the wire the whole party was to withdraw.

Signals.   All signals were by wire Buzzed or spoken and by lamp.

The Officers in charge of the assaulting parties were Lieut. DIXON J.G. and Lieut. MELHUISH J.W.D.
Officer in charge of covering party Capt. WOOD H.G.W.
also Capt. B.C.O. SHERIDAN (Medical Officer attached to the Battalion)

PROGRESS OF ASSAULT.

12.35 a.m.	The covering party under Capt. H.G.W. WOOD moved out.
1. a.m.	The covering party reported they were in position and that telephone communication had been established from the covering party to Capt. H.W. ADSHEAD at the road Barricade (K.17.c.5.1.) and the artillery central observation Post.
1. 5. a.m.	The Assaulting party under Lieut. J.G. DIXON and J.W.D. MELHUISH moved out.
1.14.a.m.	Lieut. J.G. DIXON reported his assaulting party in position.
1.17.a.m.	Capt. WOOD reported the Tape had been laid and gave the "all ready" signal.
1.17½.a.m.	Guns opened slow dropping fire.
1.24.a.m.	Reported that 1st. BANGOLORE torpedo had been fired.
1.31.a.m.	Reported that 4 Bangolores had been fired.
1.37.a.m.	R.E. reported they were unable to cut the wire right through.
1.47.a.m.	Capt. ADSHEAD reported Assaulting Party falling back.
1.50 a.m.	Assaulting Party and R.E. reported all in.
2.0. a.m.	Covering party reported all in, Artillery ceased fire.

Casualties.

1. R.E. Corpl. Shocked.
4. .. s wounded.
1. Sergt. 7th Bn. The Worcestershire Regt. wounded.

Advance.   The covering and assaulting parties moved into position without any opposition from the enemy.
The tape up to the German wire giving the line of advance was also laid without any trouble, but it would appear appear that it was not quite at a right angle to the German wire which increased slightly the amount of wire to be cut.

Wire Cutting. The R.E. worked very gallantly and quickly, their handling of the Torpedoes showed that they had been very carefully drilled, as there was no hitch in getting each Torpedo into position.
The 3rd Torpedo failed to explode so they allowed 60

Scheme for raid on trenches contd.

Wire cutting Contd.
60 seconds interval in lieu of 26 seconds then placed the 4th in position, then the 5th., both of which exploded, but in doing so it appears the 3rd which had failed partially exploded, the 6the 6th was then put in position but also failed to explode.
Actual amount of wire cut is estimated at 60 feet leaving only another 15 feet to cut which had the Torpedoes all exploded would have been easily demolished The lane cut was absolutely cleared of all wire and obstacles and was estimated at 10 to 12 feet wide.

Artillery.
The artillery barrage was very well controlled and directed and done according to prearranged plan(I make no mention of the rate of fire etc.).

Remarks.
Great credit is due to the R.E. for the way in which they worked, particularly in view of the fact that the first R.E. put out of action was the Corpral.
Captain B.C.W. SHERIDAN the Medical Officer attached to this Battalion accopanied the covering party and rendered invaluable assistance in bringing in and attending to the wounded, he actually carried one man in from in front of the covering party, the collecting and recovering of the wounded was largely due to this Officers personal energy and supervision.
The evacuation of the wounded was done by an R.A.M.C. detachment from the Field Ambulance in HEBUTERNE.

Enemy Attitude.
The enemy offered no resistance at the point of assault and only retaliated with a few shrapnel on the assaulting party and 1st Road Barricade also with some H.E. on the Battery positions.
The enemy threw up no VERY lights until after the artillery had opened fire about 5 minutes and these fell well on the flanks of the assaulting party.
They also appeared to be using a new form of rocket which ressembled a "dud" rocket and no explosion was noticed.

Lieut. Col.,
Commanding 7th Bn The Worcestershire Regiment.

16-6-16.

Scheme for Raid by 7th Battalion the Worcestershire Regiment,
Night 28/29th June, 1916.

Point of exit from our own trenches, approximately K.17.a.0.5.
Objective: K.17.b.0.2.

PLAN OF ATTACK.

Two strong bombing parties of a N.C.O. and 8 men each followed by 4 men carrying Bangalore Torpedoes followed by a covering party commanded by CAPT. H.G.W. WOOD of 19 other ranks, followed again by the two assaulting parties unders LIEUTS. J.G. DIXON and J.W.D. MELHUISH; CAPT. ADSHEAD and a weak platoon remaining behind at the point of exit in reserve.
Two Lewis Guns being posted about 200 yards in front of our own trenches well to the flanks.
1 officer, two men, and a guide were supplied by the 5th Bn. Royal ~~Royal~~ Warwickshire Regt.
A tape was laid from the point of exit to the covering party and eventually to close up to the German wire.
Telephones were arranged for and cable laid from the point of exit to the covering party.

OBJECTS.

To ascertain the damage done to the enemy wire.
To destroy as much enemy wire as possible.
To bring in identification.
To find out in what strength the enemy is holding his first and second lines.

ARTILLERY.

The Artillery arrangements were as follows:-

Watches were first sychronised.
1. That the infantry be in position half way across "no man's land" about K.17.a.5.4. by 1-15 a.m.

2. That the infantry move by the clock at 1-30 a.m. straight to the point of entry K.17.b.0.2.

1st Barrage.
At 1 a.m. two batteries to open a shrapnel barrage in front of enemy wire (not exceeding 50 yards) from point K.17.b.0.6. (road) to K.17.d.1½.9.
Rate of fire: B.F. 40 seconds.

2nd Barrage.
At 1-25 a.m. the two guns on either flank to lift on to enemy front line trench and the four centre guns to lift about 250 yards on to selected points and so form a pocket.
Rate of fire: 1-25 to 1-40 a.m. B.F. 40 seconds.
             1-40 to 1-50 a.m. B.F. 20 seconds.
             1-50 to 2-30 a.m. B.F. 40 seconds.
A section of Howitzers to bombard 2 selected points K.17.b.2.8 and K.17.b.6½.1½. i.e. Junction of trenches.

I also arranged that without I asked the artillery for any alteration to range during the second barrage that their fire would automatically stop at 2-30 a.m. 29th.

RESULT.

The Enterprise was a complete failure, due to various causes, namely:-

(a) No one in the party knew the ground.

(b) No previous reconnaissance was possible owing to short notice given.

(c) Two of the guides lost their way and did not know their way through their own wire.

(d) Owing to (c) the party had to cut their way through their own wire.

(e) The hour fixed was 1-30 a.m. but party was not in position till 2-10 a.m., due to (c) and (d).

(f) Daylight came at 3 a.m. so party had to withdraw.

DEDUCTIONS.

(a) Enemy were holding their front line in force at this point: also had cross fire from two machine guns playing on point of entry: also heavy rifle fire from front line trench.

(b) Enemy were on the alert, as at 2-15 a.m. they kept as many as 4 Very Lights in the air over the spot.

(c) Enemy wire is good along this piece of front.

The party were back in our own trenches soon after 3-30 a.m. It was then fairly light.

ARTILLERY.

The artillery worked to arranged programme, but the rate of fire was too slow, so at 1-15 a.m. it was increased to B.F. 20" and at 1-20 a.m. to 10" B.F.

COMMUNICATION.

Owing to there not being sufficient time available, no telephone was working between the point of exit and Battalion H.Q. or Artillery O.P.

6 a.m.
29/6/16.

144th Inf.Bde.
48th Div.

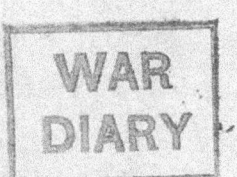

1/7th BATTN. THE WORCESTERSHIRE REGIMENT.

J U L Y

1 9 1 6

144th Brigade
48th Division

1/7th BATTALION

WORCESTERSHIRE REGIMENT

AUGUST 1 9 1 6

144th Brigade.
48th Division.

1/7th BATTALION

WORCESTERSHIRE REGIMENT

SEPTEMBER 1916

144th Brigade.

48th Division.

1/7th BATTALION

WORCESTERSHIRE REGIMENT

OCTOBER 1 9 1 6

144th Brigade.

48th Division.

1/7th BATTALION

WORCESTERSHIRE REGIMENT

NOVEMBER 1 9 1 6

144th Brigade.

48th Division.

1/7th BATTALION

WORCESTERSHIRE REGIMENT

DECEMBER 1 9 1 6

APP. B.

Report on Fighting Patrol sent out by
1/7th Bnz The Worcestershire Regt., near
The BUTTE DE WARLENCOURT.

Reference 48th Division Blue Print, Edn.4 - 1/10,000.

During the nights 1/2 and 2/3 December 1916, enemy posts were located as accurately as possible in the BUTTE TRENCH and around the BUTTE.
From the reports obtained it was thought that the enemy was holding his line with a series of small posts situated approximately at :-

    M.17.a.3545.   M.17.a.1045.
    M.17.a.3035.   M.17.a.0550.
    M.17.b.15.   M.17.a.63.-
            M.17.a.53.

The objectives decided on were:-

    To rush, kill or capture the German posts at
    approximately M.17.a.63. M.17.a.53.

Brigade fixed the time at 4 a.m. on 4/12/16 so as to coincide with a fighting patrol sent out from the Centre Battalion at the same time.
The fighting patrol was made up of 1 Officer (Lieut. G.R.WALLACE) and 20 O.R. with a covering party of 1 Officer (2/Lieut. H.G.W. TIMBRELL) with a Lewis Gun and 10 men. Both parties were all volunteers and keen to go.
The Artillery support asked for was :-

Zero to +2 mins.   A rapid barrage by field guns with H.E.
                      on BUTTE TRENCH from M.17.a.74 to M.17.a.3525.

+2 mins to +12 mins. A box barrage by field guns with H.E.
                      from M.17.b.1055 thence along GIRD
                      LINE to M.17.a.4565 to M.17.a.34.

Zero to +16 mins.   1 Battery 4.5 Hows. on M.17.a.1045 and
                      M.17.a.44.
                      (Suspected M.Gs.)

and this was arranged with the 72nd Bde. R.F.A; Col.STERLING the F.Art. Bde Commander himself kindly coming to Battalion H.Q.
On account of the difficulty of movement near the front line in daylight and the absence of prominent landmarks other than the BUTTE it is difficult to specify very accurately on the map, points on the ground.
After the frost there has been a slight thaw and this has made the forward area extremely sticky and very difficult going, especially on a dark night like that of 3/4 Dec.

NARRATIVE.
At 3.45 a.m. every man was in position about 75 yards in front of MAXWELL TRENCH about M.17.a.81.
The fighting patrol was divided into 3 parties: the left party A/C.S.M. JONES and 4 O.R. Centre party Lieut. G.R.WALLACE Cpl. COPE and 6 O.R. Right party Cpl. CUTLER and 4 O.R.
At about 12 midnight a reconnoitring patrol went out to locate the objective exactly: they were spotted and fired upon.

                                                The/......

(2)

The Artillery opened up according to programme at 4 a.m. and the patrol at once moved forward endeavouring to keep as close as possible to our barrage, which must have been accurate and effective as there was little M.G. fire and few very lights.

Part of the left party reached the left of the German post at M.17.a.65 (A).

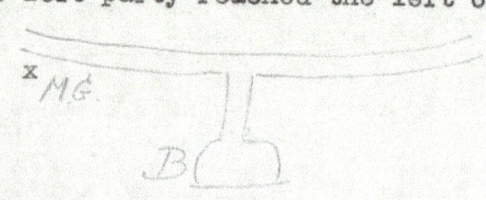

and effected an entry, and killed at least 1 man. The enemy however had time to stand to and were enfilading the left party from a sap head or shell hole (B).

Lieut. G.R. Wallace with the centre party appears to have grasped the situation and some of his party effected an entry at "B" where Cpl. COPE killed 2 Germans with his first bomb. Several of this centre party were hung up in the mud and arrived late, but a large number of bombs were thrown into the trench.

The enemy were by this time putting up a bomb barrage, and they had a M.G. in action from somewhere about M.17.a.4545, and an enemy post about M.17.a.3045 opened up with rifle fire.

The 2 parties of ours at "A" and "B" having thrown all their bombs and being outnumbered, Lieut. WALLACE withdrew them in good order to the covering party. The right portion of the fighting patrol appear to have been delayed by the thick mud and were not up in time for the encounter.

The posts at "A" and "B" are estimated at not less than 10 men in each with a M.G. at "A"; this M.G. appears to have opened fire as our party retired, but I cannot be sure of this.

Our casualties were 5 wounded and 2 have not yet reported but responsible men say they have seen both these men in our lines since the encounter.

A report will be rendered as to this as soon as possible which will probably not be before dark.

At about 4.20 a.m. the enemy were putting up a very heavy barrage on our front line and just behind it.

The failure of the patrol to obtain an identification or prisoners is due to the very bad going which casued the weaker men to fall behind and did not give us the necessary numerical superiority or equality at the point of impact.

Lieut. G.R. WALLACE appears to me to have acted with great gallantry and his arrangements for the patrol were made with care and skill, especially as for the last few days henhas been making preparations for an attack on the BUTTE.

2/Lieut. TIMBRELL i/c of the covering party carried out his duty in an able manner and with A/C.S.M. JONES and Pte. GRIFFITHS fetched in the wounded, who were quickly attended to by Captain SHERIDAN M.O. i/c 7th Worc.

The portion of the BUTTE Trench entered was in good condition and floor boarded but no revetting or firestep. The mud between the lines was extremely bad.

I wish to bring the names of the following to the notice of the Brigadier General Commdg., for gallantry displayed :-

        Lieut. GEOFFREY R. WALLACE.
        2829. Sergt. A.H. JONES A/C.S.M.
        3167. Cpl. COPE H.
            Pte. SIMCOX (who carried on though wounded in the knee at the start).
            Pte. SILAS GRIFFITHS.

The 72nd Bde. R.F.A. carried out their programme with great accuracy and skill; there were no "shorts" and from the feebleness of the enemy infantry fire it throught that the barrage was very effective.

4/12/16. 9.40 a.m.
                                  sd/ F.M. Tomkinson, Lt.-Col. Commdg.,
                                  7th Bn. Worcester Regt.

Map No 1.

Map to illustrate the operations of 1/8 Bn. The Worcestershire Regt. on the morning of 13th April 1917.

Dispositions as taken over from 1/8 Bn. The Worcestershire Regt. marked in Red
Objective gained marked thus =

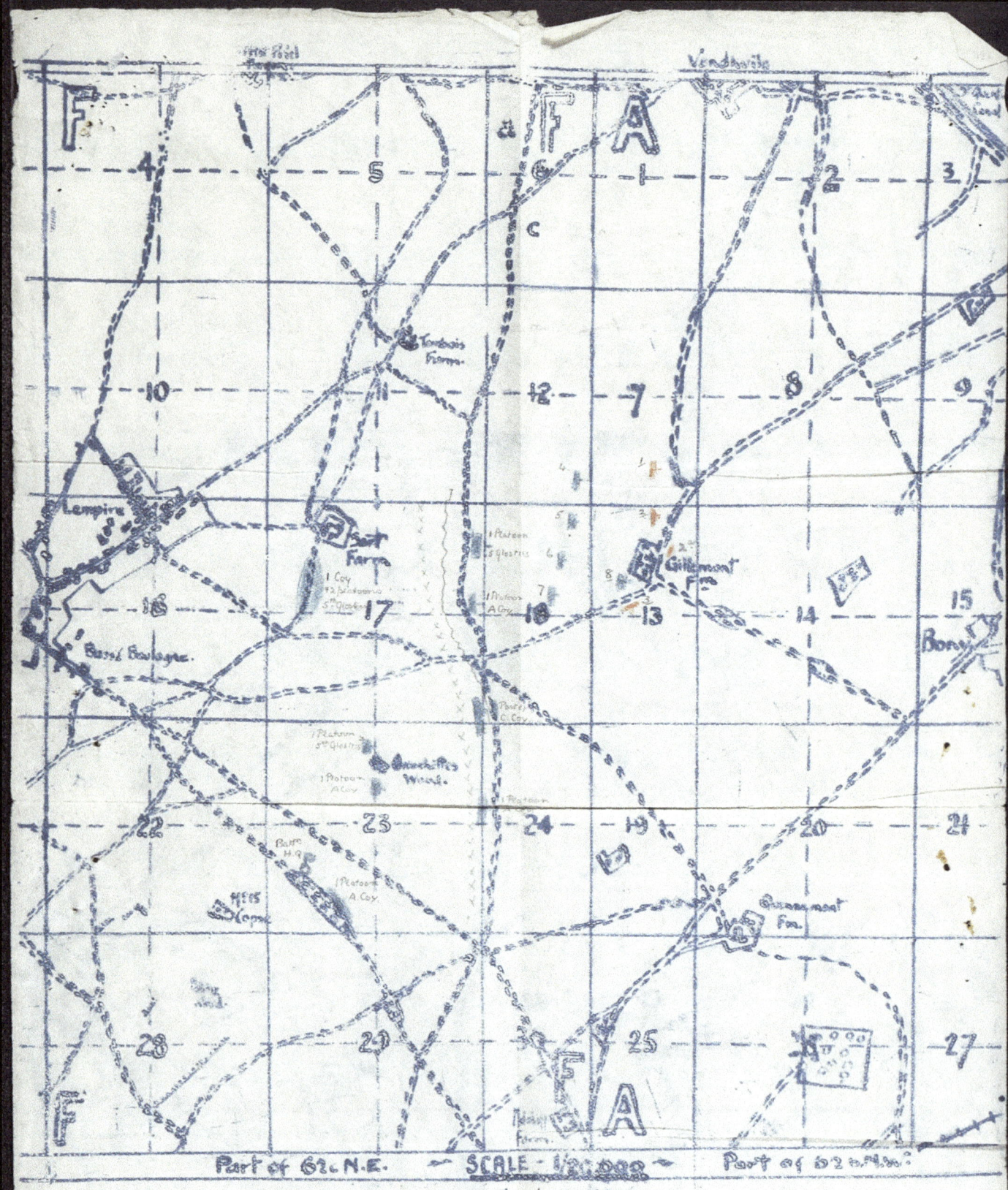

Map showing positions of troops during operations as follows:—

Post 1, 2, & 3 marked in Red were abandoned when the first enemy counter-attack took place at 6 a.m. 2nd Advanced post held by Sergt. DARBY.

The remainder of the positions, marked in BLUE show the positions held by the 7th Worcestershire Rgt. & the two attached Coys. of the 5th Gloucestershire Rt. at 9 a.m on the morning after the attack.

OPERATIONS AGAINST EPEHY 30-31 MARCH, 1.2.3 APRIL 1917.

30th. March.
At 7.30. p.m. the C.O. was sent for to Brigade. He received orders that the Battalion was to move that night to SAULCOURT WOOD and bivouac.

The Battalion with L.G. Limbers A.A.A., 5 Lewis Gun Hand Carts, 2 Water Carts, 1/2 Limber of Tools, 1 Mess Cart, Medical Cart, and 4 Cookers moved at 10.15 p.m. Major H.W. ADSHEAD had between 8 and 10 p.m. reconnoitred the road and 2/Lieut LEAKE had taken on a small advance party.

The march was via TINCOURT WOOD to LONGAVESNES to SAULCOURT WOOD.

Battalion were all in about 2.am. The night was very cold and there was little or no shelter.

31st. March.
In the morning the C.O. and Company Commanders reconnoitred a line of advance with a view to an attack on Southern end of EPEHY. The position was carefully considered from the high ground at E.11.c.55.

At 1 p.m. Brigade Order No.162 was received directing that at 5.p.m. the Battalion were to send out 2 patrols each of 1 platoon to work forward and gain the line E.13a-E12. central to E.5. central. O.C. "C" Company, Capt BUTCHER was ordered to find these patrols.

These two platoons moved out of the SAULCOURT WODD at 5.p.m. and proceeded towards their objective, whilst our guns opened up on EPEHY. (About this time the Brigade O.P. at about E.21.b.18 was heavily shelled for about half an hour and the Brigadier and the Brigade Major appeared to be in considerable danger)

2/Lieut CAMPBELL was in charge of the 2 Platoons whilst Capt BUTCHER was established at E.11 c.55 to which point a telephone line was with some difficulty laid.

When the Patrols crossed the ridge in E.17 they immediately came under Artillery fire, the advance continued but the shelling became intense 4 O.R. were killed and 6 wounded and it was impracticable to proceed. 2/Lieut CAMPBELL withdrew his patrols behind the ridge. Capt BUTCHER reported the situation to Headquarters and arranged to have another attempt at the objective at dusk. By about 8.p.m. the patrols had established themselves and were digging in on a line about 12.d. central to 12 central.

2/Lieut P.P. EDWARDS was then ordered to take up to 12 central 1,~~2000~~ /6,000 rounds of S.A.A. which at 1 a.m. he reported as done.

Meanwhile at about 7.15 p.m. the C.O. had seen the Brigade Staff and at about 7.45 p.m. operation order 162 was dictated to Adjutants of 7th. Worcs. and 6th. Gloucesters by the Brigade Major.

Earlier in the afternoon the Battalion had sent one Company to VILLERS FAUCON to work for 4th Gloucesters, this Company ("D" Coy.) returned to Saulcourt Wood at about 10.30pm

The following operation order was then issued:-
 Midnight 31/1 April 1917
Operation Order No.1. by Lieut Col. F.M. TOMKINSON D.S.O.
Commanding 1/7th. Bn. The Worcestershire Regiment.
Reference. 1/40000 Sheet 62c Edition 2.
1. 144 and 143 Infantry Brigades each with 2 Battalions less one Company for each Battalion will attack EPEHY on morning 1st April. 144 Brigade on right 143 Brigade on left.
2. For 144 Brigade 7th Worcesters will be on right of 6th Gloucesters on left dividing line between Battalions VILLERS-FAUCON - EPEHY road through E.12 Central.
The right of the 7th Worcesters will not go east of the Railway in E.23., E.18., F7., F1.
3. The Battalion will be in position with the leading Company on the line Railway at E.18.d.38. - E.18 a 33 at 5 a.m., and the advance will commence at that time.

Order of Companies B.A.D. Each Company on a 2 Platoon front, distance between lines as on diagram just issued. Distance between companies 300x

4. There will be no artillery fire during the advance unless called for by S.O.S. signal or through Battalion Headquarters.

The S.O.S. will only be fired by direct order of O.C. company or the C.O. and will not be fired unless the advance is actually held up by machine gun or heavy rifle fire.

On the S.O.S. being fired guns will open on front of EPEHY village and on the trenches immediately west of it. Fire will be kept up for 5 minutes. If more fire is wanted another S.O.S. must be sent up under the same restrictions.

At 6.30 a.m. the guns will lift beyond the village on to the line MALASSISE FM - Level crossing in F.1.b - Station and a slow fire maintained for 40 minutes unless S.O.S. is again sent up.

Companies will carry white Signal flags to call up on reaching EPEHY if weather permits.

5. A contact aeroplane will come over at 7 a.m. or one hour after the mist lifts. Flares for communication will be carried.

6. Touch will be kept with 8th Worcesters along the west of Railway line in E.8. and F.7.

7. A Brigade visual signal station will be established near wood at E.17 a 50.

8. Regular formations will be avoided and all possible use made of the ground. Sections will not be extended until visible to the enemy or fired at by machine guns or heavy rifle fire.

9. When the objective had been attained it will be consolidated forthwith against counter attack from N.E., E., and S.E.

10. Our patrols are holding a line F.13a - E.12 central where they are digging in. Endeavour is being made to form an S.A.A. dump there.

Companies will move off by platoons passing, starting point at E.15.c.83 with B company leading at 2 a.m.

11. Company Commanders will have their horses taken to the Banks about E.16.d.47, and pack animals to the same place

12. Battalion Headquarters will move at head of "D" Company.

13. Tools will be issued in separate message from Bn. Hqrs.

14. Regimental Aid Post will be at, and Field Ambulance will clear from Sunken Road about E.16.c.23.

15. Each Company will only take 4 Officers into action the remainder will report to Major ADSHEAD at Battalion Headquarters.

16. O.C. "C" Company may withdraw his 2 platoons now in front of the outpost line but only when the last line of "D" Company is 100 yards clear of these platoons.

Under no circumstances will these platoons be withdrawn while other troops are moving through them.

Copy No.1 retained.
    2 to 144 Brigade for information.
    3 to 8th Gloucesters for ditto.
    4)
    5) O.C. Companies.
    6)
    7)
    8 -to O.C. 8th. Worcesters for information.

(Signed) R.W. NIELD Captain.
Adjt. 1/7th. Bn. The Worcestershire Regiment.

April 1st

Meanwhile more tools had been obtained from the Transport and were issued to Companies. The Battalion moved off by platoons at 2 a.m. and preparatory formation was taken up correct and without incident. The time allowed was ample.

At 5 a.m. the advance commenced. ~~At ... marched ... angles into ... The~~ At this time it was very dark and distances and intervals became somewhat cramped.

At about 5.45 a.m. the leading lines entered the village. The attack was a complete surprise to the enemy who did not realise the attack until our leading lines were within 50 yards of the village: one single white very light was then sent up and

and rifle and machine gun fire opened up at once. Within 10 minutes the enemy put up a weak barrage behind all our Battn. this barrage then moved on to the S.W. edge of the village and the shelling became intense and continued intense all day at intervals. The South end of the village and F.7.a. receiving particular attention from guns of all calibres up to and including 5.9's.

At about 5.45 a.m. Battalion Headquarters was in sunken road at E.18.b.77 adjoining Headquarters 6th Gloucesters.

The situation was not clear so the C.O. sent 2/Lieut LEAKE up the road to clear it up. He saw Capt. PRESCOTT, O.C. the leading company, returned to the C.O. who sent off the following message by runner to Brigade:-

Headquarters, 144 Brigade.
Situation at 6.45 a.m.
    My first Company have reached the Railway in F.1.b. and have entered and are in the village in F.1.d.
    My second Company are partly in F.1.b. partly in F.1.d and whereabouts of remainder are unknown.
    My third Company are in a trench in F.1.c. and d.
    The enemy met our advance with rifle and machine gun fire, which was at times heavy. We were most troubled from MOLASSISE FM. which held up our right until 6.30 a.m. when the guns silenced the fire from the farm. Enemy also put up some wild shelling most of it was behind all our troops though some good shooting was done on E.6.D.3.
(second) Can give no estimate of casualties through I know there are some. I write from inter Battalion boundary road in E.18.d.
    I am now going to move to a trench in F.1. c and d and try to clear up the situation. There is no hostile rifle fire from the village.

    7.7. a.m.   (Signed) E.M. TOMKINSON
                                                          Lieut. Col,

The village was carried at the first rush and thereafter was avoided as had been ordered.

The approximate positions of units of 2 leading companies and also of 2 platoons of "D" company when the village had been passed were as under;-

(The details of other units, who had become detached and fallen on with us, are disregarded here)
(1) Some of "B" Company (Lieut. CLARK) and parts of each of "A" Coy's left platoons went approximately along road through village in F.1.c. crossed main LEMPIRE.RD. and could find no possible fire position short of the Railway Embankment about F.1.b.53. to F.1.d.88. which they occupied A few casualties were received from M.G's during this incident
(11) "B" Company under Captain PRESCOTT occupied and advanced beyond the depression N. of the road in F.1.d.35 (since known as the fort) A companies right platoon (No.4) crossed road on his right and extended his line to the Railway just N. of the level crossing. Right rear platoon (No.2) halted on the road and formed a defensive flank along Railway on F.7.b. where they were joined by a party of "D" Company Under 2/Lieut TIMBRELL. Another party of "D" company and the rest of "A" company came into the fort behind "B" company and 2 platoons "D" company were in trench in F.1.c.
(See Sketch Map. No.1.)

The above seems to have been the rough disposition. But excitement was high the situation on our left was doubtful and there was a good deal of rifle fire. Some light T.M's were being fired into the road and into the QUARRY.

Many of the enemy were seen retiring especially in the direction of MALASSISE FM. where men carrying M.G's were seen.

The enemys general position opposite us was along the 2nd railway embankment F.2.cm.F.8.a. from which he was firing sharply He also had fire positions in other places.

O.C. "A" Company did not see his way to support "B" company beyond the line of the FORT - along LEMPIRE Rd - LEVEL CROSSING and gave orders for this line to be consolidated and all parties forward of it retired.

O.C. "A" Company heard at 6.15 a.m. of the position held by "B" company and his left platoons on the Railway (Patrols, one under 2/Lieut Bundy, had been unable to find them before) In view of our 6.30 barrage O.C. "A" company ordered them to retire at once. They had started to do so already; they came back on to the road at entrance to village about F.1.d.25.

Men were now very thick on the forward position, and O.C. "A" Company sent Lieut D.G. LITTLE with most of "D" Company, some of "B" and others, to re-organise on the quarry, S. of the road

There were many wounded brough IN about this time.

During our barrage the position was organised for defence. As far as possible "A" company took over the front line, and other parties reorganised in the QUARRY behind.

At 7.10 a.m. O.C. "A" company arranged with 2/Lieut CLARK to re-occupy the embankment in F.1.b/d with his platoon. This was done

At the same time O.C. "A" company sent forward two strong ~~strong~~ patrols to occupy MALASSISE FM. This they did with some casualties, since, although the farm itself was not held, M.G's covered their approaches to it. Sergeant Langford of "D" Company was in charge of these patrols.

At 7.40am. the situation became quieter.

At 7.15 a.m. Battalion Headquarters moved forward to a trench about F.1.c.31. About 7.30 a.m. M.O. reported at Battalion Headquarters, The wounded were coming in freely: an aid post was established about F.1.c central.

At 8.30 a.m. Captain WALLACE reported in detail the position to the C.O. who then went round the line.

About this time a message of congratulation from the Brigadier to the Battalion was received. *following message was sent to Bde at 9.50am* Headquarters 144 Infantry Brigade.

I have just inspected my front line. We have an observation post at MALASSISE FARM, a post on the level crossing at E.1.d.80. One platoon with a very good fire position at F.1.d.31. Two platoons in a good position at about F.1.d.76 One platoon along railway in F.1.b. in touch with 6th Glos. (Some of the Gloucesters who were in with us are moving over to join their Battalion: this was about ½ a platoon who were at F.1.d.76.
Our front line is being steadily shelled but not accurately *by* Field Guns and Howitzers.
I think a 77 mm battery is firing from X.29.c.80.)
Remaining two companies I am placing as follows:--
2 platoons in trench F.1.c.32., 2 platoons in trench in F.12.d.. One company in sunken road running S.W. to N.E. in E.12.
My Battalion Headquarters are in a trench at F.1.c.32.
I am avoiding the village entirely as it is steadily shelled. I have seen the Germans digging in along ridge running south from X.28.c.50 25 so far as I can locate it Herewith identity Disc from German killed today at F.1.d.76. I have only collected one enemy M.G. Gun though 2 have been reported to me as captured by us.

9.50.a.m.   (Signed) F.M. TOMKINSON.
                            Lieut. Col,

"B" Company were gradually withdrawn to sunken road in E.12.b.

Throughout the day steady shelling continued: in the afternoon we were ordered to take over from 6th Gloucesters the line held by them: this was done by "C" Company who had been in SAULCOURT WOOD since 6.30 a.m. and was carried out without incident, and the necessary readjustment of supports and reserves was made. Battalion Headquarters moved to F.1.oo, and rations and water were brought there by limber.

One Machine Gun and two Lewis Guns were captured by "A" company from the enemy.

17 dead Germans were counted in our area and much equipment was abandoned.

During the night on orders from Brigade MALASSISE FARM was consolidated by one platoon of "D" company, and patrols pushed out to keep touch with the enemy. The vicinity of the Regimental

Aid Post and the south end of the village were very heavily shelled at intervals in the night.
  Casualties : 1 Officer (2/Lieut FELLOWS) and 9 O.R. killed) 40 Other ranks wounded.

T.P.1.
  Headquarters.,   2nd April 1917
   144 Infantry Brigade.
  Herewith sketch of dispositions.
  The main line of resistance is shewn by the coloured marks. In addition to this patrols and group sentries are posted forward at different points

  Map shewing dispositions of 1/7th. Bn. The Worcestershire Regiment on night 1/2 April 1917. Right company in Blue, left company in Red.

Scale 1/20,000   (Signed) F.M. TOMKINSON.
             Lieut. Col. 7th. Worcesters.

T.P.2.
  Headquarters.,
   144 Infantry Brigade.   2nd April 1917.
  Reference attached.
  The general arrangement is:-
Outpost line -
  On the right. One company with one platoon in
    MALASSISE FARM.
  On the left. One company.
  Each company finding its own support except that the left company has one platoon of one of the Reserve companies at his disposal in case of alarm.
  In reserve. Two companies less one platoon.

2. p.m.   (Signed) F.M. TOMKINSON.
            Lt. Col, 7th. Worcesters.
2nd. April,
  The C.O. and the Brigade Major went along the front line about 7.15 a.m.
  The day was somewhat quieter though towards evening front line and MOLASSISE FARM were heavily shelled, and the village received attention all day.
  At dark the two front companies were relieved without incident by the remaining two companies.
3rd April,
  The G.O.C. Division visited Battalion Headquarters, and made a personal survey of the country beyond our lines. He congratulated the Battalion on their work.

The shelling was much less violent during the day, and it was now possible to use the village with more safety. Captain CRAWFORD (R.E.) inspected in the early morning some suspected mines in the billets of "B" company and the Aid Post. He also searched the HOSPICE CAMUS and the POST OFFICE which were reported by prisoners to be mined.

The Battalion was relieved in the evening by the 1/5th Gloucesters. Relief began about 9.p.m. and the platoons when freed marched to SAULCOURT WOOD where tea was served. After a halt the Battalion marched away to HAMEL near TINCOURT into good billets. Relief being complete by 3.15 a.m. The last part of the march was done in heavy rain, but the men finished splendidly.

Summary of Patrols sent out during Operations.

a. On night of 1/2nd, 2nd Lieut LLOYD and a patrol consisting of one platoon of "D" Company pushed out to MALASSISE FARM and remained there until relieved by 2nd Lieut TIMBRELL the next night. He was shelled at intervals and fairly heavily when the guns opened on RONSSOY previous to the 8th Worcesters sending out their patrols towards that village. He saw small enemy patrols during the day but expressed the opinion that barring these patrols there were no Germans within 3,000 yards of his post. He also reported a trench with wire near the EPEHY-RONSSOY road in F.3.b.75.

b. This post was relieved by 2nd.Lieut TIMBRELL on the evening of the 2/3rd. He sent out a patrol to explore the copse at F.9.c. Nothing was seen or heard of the enemy but two disused sentry boxes were found and also a dummy battery. This patrol also came into touch with a patrol of 8th.Worcesters.

c. A patrol was sent out from MALASSISE FARM at 4.30.a.m. on morning of 3rd inst to examine the trench at F.3.b.2. They did not enter the trench and failed to find any trace of the enemy.

OPERATIONS OF THE 1/7th. BATTALION THE WORCESTERSHIRE REGIMENT

16th. - 17th. AUGUST 1917.

ZERO for the attack by the 145th. Infantry Brigade on the German positions East of the STEENBEEK was at 4-45 a.m. 16th.   This Battalion was under orders to have one Coy. on the STEENBEEK at zero plus 3 hours, and the remaining Coys. in O.B.1. and O.G.1 by zero plus 5.

At 4-30 a.m. Battalion Headquarters moved to O.G.2. near Civilization Farm, "D" Coy moved East of HUGEL HALLES.   A Battalion O.P. was established to the left of OBLONG FARM.

The remaining three Coys. crossed the CANAL at 6-45 a.m., and moved to positions as ordered.

We were not able to obtain any definite information either from Division or our own O.P.   At 6-35 a.m. enemy barrage was heavy on the STEENBEEK and KITCHENER'S WOOD line.

At 11 a.m. orders were received from Division to move the Battalion to a position of readiness EAST of the STEENBEEK, because left Division had reported that their right had lost direction, and was not in touch with our left.

Still no definite news from the front.

At 11-30 a.m. the Battalion commenced to move as follows:-
"D" Coy. EAST of the STEENBEEK in C 11 B.
"C" Coy. Between the STEENBEEK and HUGEL HALLES.
"B" Coy. about ALBERTA.
"A" Coy. about CANOPUS support.
Battalion Headquarters at C. 11 A. 66 near REGINA CROSS.

From reconnaissance, particularly by Captain Lloyd M.C. it appeared that the 145th. Brigade had made very little ground on our front, that they were badly held up in front of MON DU HIBOU and HILLOCK FARM; that they had captured no part of the LANGEMARCK - GHELUVELT line, and had except for some small isolated parts been driven back on the STEENBEEK where they held a very irregular line never more than two or three hundred yards EAST of the STEENBEEK.

During the move up of this Battalion shelling was very heavy, and remained very heavy for the next twelve hours, particularly on the line REGINA CROSS to ALBERTA.   Aimed rifle fire from the German posts also caused casualties.   On the other hand our leading troops found a number of good rifle targets which were dealt with to good effect.

The general position was reported to Brigade by message timed 1-45 p.m.

At 4-15 p.m. orders were received from Brigade to reconnoitre with a view to attacking MON DU HIBOU at dusk.

At 6-20 p.m. orders were received to capture strong post at TRIANGLE FARM VANCOUVER and MON DU HIBOU without artillery preparation.

A telephone message had been received at 5-15 p.m. forecasting this operation.   At 6-7 p.m. O.C. "C" Coy. received his orders to carry this out.   His Coy. was at that time dug in on the WEST Bank of the STEENBEEK in 11 B.   Zero was 7-30 p.m.

At zero "B" Coy. were to move from ALBERTA to the WEST Bank of the STEENBEEK and "A" Coy. were to move up to ALBERTA.

At zero "C" Coy. advanced to the attack, they immediately came under heavy rifle and machine gun fire from the German positions on their right and from MON DU HIBOU; their leading wave was nearly all wiped out.   Captain Montgomery was shot through the stomach, and Lieut. Haslewood was shot through the knee.   "D" Coy. had endeavoured to provide covering fire with Lewis Guns, but the rifle and machine gun fire from the German positions on the right made this very difficult. 2/Lieut. Gadsby assisted by Coy. Sergeant Major Mole took over the Coy. and dug in about 350 yards EAST of the STEENBEEK and facing MON DU HIBOU.

A telephone message was received from Brigade about 11 p.m. and confirmed by wire received at 1-20 a.m. to renew the attack with zero at 2-30 a.m. and with a standing barrage on the objectives for this operation "B" Coy. was moved from the STEENBEEK into "C" Coy's position in front of MON DU HIBOU, and the latter moved back to the STEENBEEK.

The attack was delivered with determination, and despite casualties some of our men reached part of the objectives.

Here 2/Lieut. H.B. Bate who had showed great courage and determination and Captain W.N.S. Brown were both badly wounded. Parties of Germans appeared with bombs and our men were driven out, and dug in with their leading line about 100 yards SOUTH WEST of MON DU HIBOU. About this time three prisoners were taken who had probably formed one of the German front posts.

2/Lieut Flower took over command of "B" Coy. and re-organized.

The evacuation of the wounded of "C" and "B" Coys. was extremely difficult, but carried out with great gallantry by stretcher bearers and others.

Through the whole of the 17th. the shelling was heavy and continuous and caused many casualties, at the same time many Germans appeared to be in a low state of morale, and some made offers to surrender to "B" Coy. which were not successful.

Communication was maintained with the Brigade throughout the whole of the operations except for very short periods and for an interval on the evening of the 17th. owing to fine work by Battalion and Brigade linesmen.

At 9-30 p.m. the relief of the Battalion by two Coys. of the 8th. Worcesters commenced, meantime the scattered and disorganized troops of the 145th. Brigade which were on our front had been so far as possible withdrawn. These troops had had a very hard time having been heavily shelled and their formation broken up before zero for their initial attack. They had been unable to keep up with the artillery barrage, and had therefore been met by very heavy rifle and machine gun fire. Their casualties however on our front were not much heavier than our own. The relief proceeded well and was complete about 11-15 p.m.

The track from ALBERTA to OBLONG FARM was very heavily shelled during most of the relief, and gas was encountered EAST of the CANAL.

The 8th. Worcesters had their Battalion Headquarters at ALBERTA, this had not been available for us because the 1/4th. Ox. and Bucks. were there.

2/Lieut J.T. Burton acted as liaison officer with the Right Battalion of the 11th. Division who were on our left, and 2/Lieut. H.G.W. Timbrell performed a similar duty with the Oxford and Bucks.

Both these officers are reported to have come under shell fire.

The Regimental Aid Post was at ALBERTA where Lieut. Milligan the Battalion M.O. did much good work.

"A" Coy. (Capt. G.R. Wallace M.C.) carried the rations from OBLONG FARM and delivered them correct under great difficulties.

Casualties. Officers 8.
Captain A.B. Montgomery since died. Captain W.N.S. Brown., 2/Lieut. R.S. Leake., 2/Lieut. G.H. Haslewood., 2/Lieut H.B. Bate., 2/Lieut W.J. Flower. Captain A.O.Lloyd M.C. & 2/Lt. R.P.Thompson were wounded and remained at duty.

Other Ranks. Killed.   21.
              Wounded.   102.
              Wounded and re-
              mained at duty.   16.
              Missing.   12.
              Total other Ranks.   151.

The Battalion moved to the CANAL BANK after relief.

The following N.C.O's and men were specially recommended by the O.C. Coys. for gallantry and devotion to duty:-

200235.	Sgt.	Conway M.C.	"A" Coy.	
200956.	Cpl.	Millward T.	"B" .	
201706.	Pte.	Shakespeare J.	"B" .	
202030.	.	Hale G.	"B" .	) Stretcher
201140.	.	Rollison S.	"B" .	) Bearers.
201581.	.	Price T.	"C" .	
300423.	.	Smith T.	"C" .	Stretcher Bearer
242448.	.	Hicks R.	"C" .	
240360.	L/Cpl.	Baxter A.	"C" .	
203206.	Pte.	Harvey A.S.	"C" .	
200268.	.	Protheroe A.	"D" .	)
201564.	.	Breeze A.	"D" .	) Stretcher
20309.	.	Chamberlain W.	"D" .	) Bearers.

The Battalion Linesmen particularly 200488 Pte. G.F. Bell, 201817 Pte. J.W. Jones, and the Battalion Runners particularly 200692 Pte. E.G. Kelly and 200498 Pte. L.A. Taylor rendered much valuable service under very difficult conditions.

Report on Operations of The 1/7th. Battalion The Worcestershire Regt.
8th.-9th.-10th. October 1917.
....

While the Battalion was in rest billets near AUDRICQ at the end of September the Brigadier-General Commanding the Brigade explained the general plan of operations by the Division and the ground over which we should have to fight, and this was so far as practicable communicated to all ranks and practised on marked ground.

On the 5th. October the Battalion marched from BRAKE CAMP to DAMBRE CAMP, and the C.O. was informed that the attack would take place at dawn on the 9th.

On the 6th. October the C.O. and Captain Harris went up near Vale House and considered the ground and the question of H.Q.

On the morning of the 7th. the Battalion moved to the CANAL BANK with the intention of moving to the line that evening and attacking on the 9th. About mid-day however heavy rain set in and continued throughout the afternoon. Brigade warned the Battalion that the Brigade would probably not move up that night and this was stated definitely about 3-30 p.m.

The 8th. broke fine and orders were issued about mid-day that we should move to the line in the evening and take up position for attack at dawn, the 4th. Royal Berks to leave an outpost Coy. to cover our assembly. A copy of Battalion orders and instructions as follows:-

Copy no   7th. Worcs. Op. Ord. No.4.   8.10.17

1. At a time to be notified later the Battn. in conjunction with 49th. Division on the right and 6th. Glosters on left will continue the offensive.
2. Boundaries and objectives are shown on attached map.
   The first objective will be attacked, captured, and consolidated by "B" Coy. on the Right and "C" Coy. on the left, and the second objective by "A" Coy. on the Right and "D" Coy. on the left.
3. O.C. Coys. will detail separate parties to deal with each known enemy strong point in their area and will also maintain a reserve against the unexpected and against counter-attack.
   As objectives are captured O.C. Coys. will thin out their front and consolidate in depth. In particular O.C. "B" Coy. will construct a strong point at ADLER FARM and O.C. "A" Coy. a strong point between VARLET FARM and WALLEMOLEN.
4. O.C. 144 Coy. M.G.C. will detail 2 M.Gs. to move in rear of "B" Coy. to assist in holding their objective at ADLER FARM and 2 M.Gs. to move in rear of "A" Coy. to assist in holding the WALLEMOLEN RIDGE.
5. The retention of the WALLEMOLEN RIDGE is of the utmost importance.
6. The Battalion will be in position with the leading troops in rear of our front line posts at zero minus 30 minutes.
   O.C. "B" and "C" Coys. will arrange for the laying out of tapes on the night previous to zero and to knot their tapes together and also knot with troops on flanks.
7. The attack will be made under an artillery barrage which will come down at zero 150 yards in front of our line lifting at zero plus 4 minutes. Up to the limit of first objective the barrage will move at 100 yards every 6 minutes when a protective barrage will be formed.
   At zero plus 1 hour 46 minutes this barrage will lift and creep forward to limit of final objective at rate of 100 yards in 8 minutes.
8. Special parties each of 1 N.C.O. and 3 men will be told off to meet similar parties from 49th. Division as follows:-
   By O.C. "B" Coy. at junction of old trenches at D 5 b 51.
   By O.C. "A" Coy. on Road N.E. of WALLEMOLEN V 28 c 20.
9. H.Q. will be as follows:-

    Brigade H.Q.   Artillery House
                        with command post at
                        ARBRE.
    6th. Glosters.   WINCHESTER.
    7th. Worcs.   VICTORIA HOUSE
                        D 7 b 32 with
                        advanced Battn. H.Q. on
                        STROOMBEEK at D 2 d 17.
and a Battalion visual station will be established at D 2 d 16

Sheet 3.

connecting with rear Battn. H.Q.
Aid Post JANET FARM.
Relay Posts will be notified by the M.O. to all concerned.
10. Acknowledge.

                           F.M. TOMKINSON Lt.-Col.
Copy 1 retained.
                              1/7th. Worcs. Regt.
2,3,4,5. Coys.
6 M.G.C.
7. 6th. Glosters.
8 Bde.
9 right Bn.
Issued 12-30 noon.

      Instructions to accompany 7th. Worcs. Op. Ord. No. 4 of 8-10-17

1. 145 Brigade will hold our front with nearly 1 Coy. until after we have passed through them.
2. 145 Brigade M.Gs will be in our front system and will engage any direct targets they see.
3. 2/Lieut. C.L. Dobner will be in charge of the Liaison posts with Right Division.
4. Four tanks may be used on our front, but in no case are troops to await the arrival of the tanks.
5. Contact aeroplanes will fly over objectives at :-
      zero plus 1 hour 30 minutes.
      zero plus 2 hours 30 minutes.
      and when ordered by Corps.
Infantry will be ready to light Red flares (in lines not in groups) at these hours but will not light flares unless called for by KLAXON HORN or dropping white lights.
6. An aeroplane to watch for enemy counter-attacks will be up continuously from zero.
Whenever this plane observes hostile parties of 100 or more moving to counter-attack it will drop a smoke bomb over that portion of the front to which the enemy is moving.
This smoke bomb will burst about 100 feet below the aeroplane into a white parachute flare which will descend slowly leaving a long trail of brown smoke about a foot broad behind it.
7. Before zero O.C. "D" Coy. will draw 20 boxes S.A.A. from the dump on corduroy track about 750 yards EAST of HORNER FARM and take them to advanced Battn. H.Q. on STROOMBEEK.
8 All Officers advancing over the open must carry rifles
9. The capture of objectives can be signalled to Battn. H.Q. as follows:-
      "B" Coys. objective W.
      "C" Coys. objective X.
      "A" Coys. objective Y.
      "D" Coys. objective. Z.
10. Wrap all rifles up as much as possible.
11. Guides to-night will be provided only for the 2 front Coys. and will be 1 per platoon: They will meet us at ARBRE.
12. Captain Butcher is taking up 1 O.R. per platoon this afternoon. O.C. Coys. will also each send up 1 Officer to do further reconnaissance and meet Coys. on arrival.
13. Coys. will move so as to pass commencement of track at Bridge 2 A as follows:-
      ½ Battn. H.Q.   4-30 p.m.
      followed by "B" "C" "D" "A"
      Coys with 100 yards between platoons.
14. Coys. will report all in position for attack by word RAT.
15. Route up tonight track from Bridge 2 A up to ADMIRAL'S ROAD then to the right along ADMIRAL'S ROAD and take JULIET FARM - SPRINGFIELD - ARBRE track.
16. It is hoped to issue before we move rations for consumption on 10th but Coys. will not wait for these.
17. 1 extra Bandolier per man will be issued under Battalion arrangements and carried.
18. Ref. para 15. 2/Lieut. Wingate will regulate traffic on ADMIRAL'S ROAD where we shall cross the Glosters who are using the ALBERTA TRACK from ADMIRAL'S ROAD.
                               F.M. TOMKINSON. Lieut-Col.
                                1/7th. Worcs. Regt.

Sheet 3.

Rations for two days were issued. 120 Tommy Cookers. 85 Autobouillants were issued to Battn. from Brigade and by Battn. to the men. 250 Tommy Cookers made under Battn. arrangements were also issued and found invaluable being preferred by the men to the Govt. issue

Captain A.H. Butcher went on in advance with 1 O.R. per platoon to reconnoitre and learn some of the ground. Heavy rain set in at 4 p.m.

The head of the Battn. left the CANAL BANK at 4-30 p.m. and moved up the MOUSETRAP - JULIET FARM - SPRINGFIELD - ARBRE trench board track.

The Divisional Commander was met on the track and spoke to the troops words of encouragement.

Battn. H.Q. went to P. House (sometimes called VICTORIA FARM) at D 7 b.38. (a concrete mebus EAST of the LANGEMARCK-GHELUVELT line) arriving there at 6-30 p.m.

The Royal Berks had only been in the sector for 1 day, they worked very hard to facilitate the assembly but it was very wet and dark and several parties went astray.

An advanced Battn. H.Q. was established on the STROOMBEEK in a mebus at D 2 d 17 with Capt. A.H. Butcher in charge.

Lieut. Hancocks and 2/Lieut. Edwards started at dusk to tape out assembly positions for the 2 front Coys.: considerable progress was made but the mud, wet and darkness made it of very little assistance.

The British front line was along the old trench from approx. D 2 b 56 to D 3 c 57: the Battalion was formed up in shell holes as far as practicable in straight lines immediately behind the front line on a depth of 300 yards : leading Coys. "B" on right "C" on left rear Coys. "A" on right "D" on left. The assembly position was so chosen with intent to miss the German barrage which was said to fall on the line of the STROOMBEEK. The assembly was completed by 2 a.m. The assembly area was shelled all night: at times violently and the Battn. suffered about 30 casualties before zero.

The rain ceased about 4 a.m. and a high wind sprang up which was bitterly cold : zero was at 5-20 a.m. which on account of the weather seemed too early as it was almost quite dark the moon being very clouded

Our barrage appeared to come down 1½ minutes before zero and commenced ragged & weak : in a few minutes it became intense: German S.O.S. went up within 2 minutes of our barrage commencing and the German barrage commenced to fall 5-22 a.m. falling well NORTH of the STROOMBEEK and right on our 2 rear Coys. killing the O.C. right rear Coy. and 1 of his Officers. The troops advanced correct as soon as our barrage began: front lines extended remainder in small columns : rear Coy on Right came forward quickly to clear the German barrage and thereby lost depth. 2 platoons of our left rear Coy. lost direction and advanced into the area of the Battn. on our left (6th. Glosters) while troops of that Battn. also advanced into our area but very little confusion was caused thereby. Before zero we were in trench on both flanks.

Immediately our barrage came down heavy rifle and M.G. fire opened up from the German front and continued notwithstanding our barrage

Enfilade fire in particular came from the direction of VACHER FARM

It was at once apparent that the Germans were holding their front line in great strength with many M.Gs. The barrage was lost at the start in fact the Battn. were never close up to it at all. the ground NORTH of the STROOMBEEK had certainly been heavily shelled but it was good going compared to the STROOMBEEK valley and ground SOUTH thereof.

The attack progressed for about 300 yards when it was definitely held up about 5-45 a.m.: by this time about 8 of the 12 Officers with Coys. were casualties.

On the left prisoners were captured at the start. About 6 a.m. "A" Coy. (right support) were ordered to push on through "B" Coy. and renewed the attack: "A" Coy. Officers were all casualties and O.C. "B" Coy. Capt. T.C.F. HARRIS personally organised and led this attack making progress eventually with some of his own men to within 50 yards of the German lines.

At this time an officer who had come over from 49th. Division to liaise was killed.

About this time rifle and Lewis Gun targets began to present themselves and the killing of Germans commenced.

About 7-30 a.m. under heavy rifle and Lewis Gun fire from our lines the Germans began to break fastly on the left and targets became better: about 40 prisoners gave themselves up at about D 3 a 08 to the Battn. on our left following immediately by two batches of about

Sheet 4.

30 each who surrendered along our front. About the same time parties of our troops entered the German front trench: this trench was eventually found to be a well constructed continuous breast work trench with wooden shelters therein but no concrete. It contained a large number of dead Germans, at least 50, and two dug-outs had had direct hits from shells and each contained 6 dead We captured in this trench 2 heavy Machine Guns, 7 Light Machine guns and a large quantity of rations.

It was noticed that by each Machine Gun there were about 3 dead mostly killed by bullets in the head.

(It is thought that some of the left front Coy. had in the initial stages penetrated beyond the German front line and that some of our men had reached about V 27 c 41 but they stayed there all day and came back about 6-30 p.m.)

As soon as the trench was taken patrols were pushed out along the front of our line: the trench had a very good view and field of fire for over 300 yards: ADLER FARM contained 1 cellar which had been knocked in and no other cover. Patrols passed beyond ADLER FARM about 10-40 a.m. and the capture of ADLER FARM was reported to Brigade at 11-16 a.m.

A large party of Germans from EAST of ADLER FARM came out to surrender, our men held up biscuits to them but they went to the Right Division.

At 11 a.m. the following was received from Brigade:-
"Brigade on right report they are about D 3 b 79
they are sending reserves to clear up situation about
D 3b.79"

This report of advance by Right Brigade was not credited by us as the Germans could be seen in numbers in trench D 3 b 11 to D 3 b 71 which was reported to gunners who however could not shoot on account of the reports of Right Brigade.

At 11-15 a.m. Brigade advised Battn. H.Q. that they were moving up 1 Coy. 8th. Worcesters to our support.

Re-organisation of the Coys. and the line was now made : the Coy. of 8th. Worcesters were put in on left in two lines, our "B" on right with "C" in support, our "A" Coy. and 2 Bde. Machine Guns (the other two had been knocked out) in the old British line and the remains of "D" Coy. formed Battn. Reserve.

The Coy. of 8th. Worcs. were ordered to make an attack on INCH HOUSES and this was arranged for 5 p.m., but at this time our guns were shelling INCH HOUSES heavily and the attack could not take place as the shelling did not lift.

Remainder of the day and all night 9/10 were fairly quiet except for a spell of brisk shelling at dusk. 2/Lieut Wingate took out a patrol to near INCH HOUSES collided with a sentry, shot him with his revolver and got clear away.

During the night cocoa, water and rum were sent up to the front line and issued correct.

The Divisional Commander sent up to Battn H.Q. through Bde. 2 bottles of Champagne and some chocolate etc.: this was consumed by Officers in the front line on early morning of 10th. and the thought and action were much appreciated.

At about 5-30 a.m. on 10th. the Germans put down a weak barrage along the ridge NORTH of STROOMBEEK, but thereafter the day was quiet. All our casualties were evacuated, and all our dead who could be found were buried.

At 6 a.m. on 10th. touch in the front line was made by us with 49th. Division at D 3 c 68 where they had a Machine Gun post and in support line touch had always been maintained at KRONPRINZ FARM: this Division did not appear to have advanced any further than we had and were in fact behind us. It is not understood how they claimed on 9th. to be at D 3 b 79.

At dusk in accordance with orders from Brigade posts each of 1 N.C.O. and 5 men were sent out approximately to D 3 a 94 : D 3 a 64 D 3 a 64 : D 3 a 26 to cover the impending relief and the line of the VACHER FARM - ADLER FARM road and such posts were handed over on relief.

The Battn was relieved in the night by 7th. Battn. Seaforth Highlanders 9th. Division who commenced to arrive at 9 p.m.

Relief was complete about Midnight and our Battn. moved to

Sheet 5.

IRISH FARM and then to CANAL BANK and to SIEGE CAMP.
We laid out a tape from the STROOMBEEK to D 3 a 3525 for a dividing line between Coys. for the relieving unit.
The bulk of our Battalion arrived at IRISH FARM at 3 a.m. and at SIEGE CAMP 8 a.m. there was some shelling of tracks on way out but not many casualties. 13 of the 16 Lewis Guns taken into action were brought out, the 3 missing ones having been destroyed.
We also handed over to 7th. Seaforth Highlanders the right Coy. front of 6th. Glosters.
Our Casualties were as follows:-

OFFICERS 10.
    Killed. Capt. R.W. HOARE, Lieut. W. HANCOCKS, Lieut. D.S.E. MILLIGAN, 2/Lieut. F.W. GOULD, 2/Lieut. H.J. EDWARDS.
    Wounded. Capt. W.C. CASSELS M.C., Capt. H.C.B. BROWN, 2/Lieut. H.R. FELTON, 2/Lieut. J.A. ACWORTH, 2/Lieut. A.F. WHORTON.

OTHER RANKS.
    Killed.   54
    Wounded. 135
    Missing   22
    Wounded and
      remained 1.
    Total   212

Answers to Questions by G.O.C. Division on Operations
9th. - 10th. - 11th. October 1917.
....

1. This Battalion assembled NORTH of the STROOMBEEK on a depth of
   300 yards, leading line from D 2 b 43 to D 3 c 16

2. By platoons from CANAL BANK.

3. About 2 a.m.

4. Yes. But were found or found themselves so as to be in position
   about 2 a.m.: in all about 4 platoons were temporarily lost
   on account of the darkness and the fact that the guides had only
   indifferent knowledge of the ground.

5. Very little rest and no organised feeding: shelling was constant
   on the assembly position after about 2 a.m.

6. Battn. H.Q. were at P. House D 7 b 32 with an advanced Battn.
   H.Q. on STROOMBEEK at D 2 d 17.

7. No. There was a very good view from Battn. H.Q. and none from
   Advanced Battn. H.Q.

8. By runner to advanced Battn. H.Q.   by lamp which worked very
   well day and night from Advanced Battn. H.Q. to Battn. H.Q. but
   this method could only be used from front to rear; messages
   to the front were sent by runner.

9. /

10. Certainly: it was very good throughout.

11. Yes. both logs were used each with important situation reports.
    Pigeons were satisfactory except one who went wrong. Lamp to
    Brigade at ARBRE was satisfactory: telephone line to Artillery
    House was maintained. Runners were also used.

12. We thought it came down 1½ minutes before zero and was weak and
    ragged at start: in about a minute it became intense and accurate
    but it never stopped the rifle and machine gun fire from the
    German lines.

13. No noticeable gap.

14. Vide answer to 12.   also 2 wooden shelters in German front line
    were found to have had direct hits, and each had 6 dead inside.

15. About 3 p.m. I asked for the S.O.S. lines to be the lines of the
    first protective barrage in the morning's attack but this could
    not be done because it was alleged that the 48th. Division were
    at D 3 b 72.

16.(a) On the left it is thought that a small party reached about V 27 c
    41 and stayed there until dusk when they withdrew, but I can't
    clear this up.
   (b) The following points were reached, maintained and handed over
    D 3 a 26, D d d 35, D d a 75, and D 3 a 94.

17. (a) Was not   (b) were.

18. As regards the small party on the left I think they withdrew
    because they were not only isolated but also lost.

19. All along the line of the German Trench.

20. A man to go or sent with stretcher parties: the prisoners were all
    used to carry wounded and without them we should have had the
    very greatest difficulty: they worked very well.

21. Captain Harris who was on the spot and I approved of it with
    addition of small posts pushed out to front.

Sheet 4.

22. Trench was re-dug about 4ft., a great quantity of German bombs were collected and placed on each post; troops were re-organised food, water, S.A.A. and rifle grenades were collected from casualties.

23. Patrols were in front but no actual covering party was needed by day because there was a splendid field of view and fire.

24. Battn. H.Q. and the sentry posts in front line; the intermediate ground offered no facilities for observation.

25. None in the initial stages, but after the barrage was lost the advance was made by fire and movement.

26. None owing to formation of ground.

27. Each rifle had one sandbag on muzzle and two around the breech until zero: Lewis Guns had special covers which had been made out of canvas under Battalion arrangements.
   After zero rifles though not unserviceable were never really capable of sustained rapid fire until they had been cleaned during the consolidation. Lewis Guns were better; one gun fired the whole of the day whenever required without a stoppage, firing over 600 rounds and ending with all his 6 pans full. He had lost 4 pans.

28. Heavy, and it was fairly accurate. Many men used up the 170 rounds they had carried up and obtained more from casualties: 16 boxes S.A.A. were sent up but not needed on account of S.A.A. from casualties.

29. I can only trace that 3 were fired: they were fired at an M.G. at about D.3.b.96 and had no appreciable effect: the Machine Gun team were subsequently killed by our rifle fire and the gun was captured.

30. No.

31. Not actually fired: by zero 2 Machine Guns out of our 4 and an equivalent of 2 teams were casualties. The other 2 guns were put in position in our reserve line on the right and were a source of great comfort. The 2 M.G. Officers with us worked hard and worked well.

32. Not on any serious scale. The small party of ours referred to in 16 scattered a small counter-attack on their left and inflicted casualties.

33. In initial stages all along their trench later in trench in D.3.b.12 to D.3.b.62: we tried to get the artillery on this target but it could not be done on account of obscure situation on the right.

34. In initial stage the leading line was extended and remainder were in section columns: later as the rifle fight developed all were in extended lines while actually fighting.

35. Yes. If there had been more the casualties before zero would probably have lowered the general morale. Owing to casualties there were not enough Officers and apart from casualties there were not enough N.C.Os with initiative.

36. Yes most satisfactory.

37. On the extreme left there were probably about 6 unburied: the number we buried was probably 66. Our burial return shows only 39.

38. At present 12.

39. No.

13/10/17.

48TH DIVISION
144TH INFY BDE

1-8TH BN WORCS REGT
APR 1915-AUG 1918.

1917 OCT

TO ITALY

144th Inf.Bde.
48th Div.

Battn. disembarked
Boulogne from
England 1.4.15.

1/8th BATTN. THE WORCESTERSHIRE REGIMENT.

A P R I L

1 9 1 5

144th Inf.Bde.
48th Div.

1/8th BATTN. THE WORCESTERSHIRE REGIMENT.

M A Y
(5.5.15 - 31.5.15)
1 9 1 5

144th Inf.Bde.
48th Div.

1/8th BATTN. THE WORCESTERSHIRE REGIMENT.

J U N E

(4.6.15 to 29.6.15)

1 9 1 5

144th Inf.Bde.
48th Div.

1/8th BATTN. THE WORCESTERSHIRE REGIMENT.

J U L Y

1 9 1 5

144th Inf.Bde.
48th Div.

1/8th BATTN. THE WORCESTERSHIRE REGIMENT.

A U G U S T

1 9 1 5

144th Inf.Bde.
48th Div.

1/8th BATTN. THE WORCESTERSHIRE REGIMENT.

S E P T E M B E R

1 9 1 5

144th Inf.Bde.
48th Div.

1/8th BATTN. THE WORCESTERSHIRE REGIMENT.

O C T O B E R

1 9 1 5

144th Inf.Bde.
48th Div.

1/8th BATTN. THE WORCESTERSHIRE REGIMENT.

N O V E M B E R

1 9 1 5

144th Inf.Bde.
48th Div.

1/8th BATTN. THE WORCESTERSHIRE REGIMENT.

D E C E M B E R

1 9 1 5

144th Brigade.

48th Division.

1/8th BATTALION

WORCESTERSHIRE REGIMENT

JANUARY 1 9 1 6

144th Brigade.
48th Division.

1/8th BATTALION

WORCESTERSHIRE REGIMENT

FEBRUARY 1 9 1 6

144th Brigade.

48th Division.

1/8th BATTALION

WORCESTERSHIRE REGIMENT

MARCH 1 9 1 6

144th Brigade.

48th Division.

———

1/8th BATTALION

WORCESTERSHIRE REGIMENT

APRIL 1 9 1 6

144th Brigade.

48th Division.

1/8th BATTALION

WORCESTERSHIRE REGIMENT

M A Y 1 9 1 6

144th Brigade.

48th Division.

1/8th BATTALION

WORCESTERSHIRE REGIMENT

JUNE 1916

144th Inf.Bde.
48th Div.

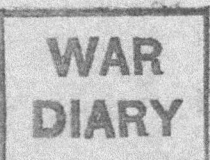

1/8th BATTN. THE WORCESTERSHIRE REGIMENT.

J U L Y

1 9 1 6

144th Brigade
48th Division

1/8th BATTALION

WORCESTERSHIRE REGIMENT

AUGUST 1916

144th Brigade.

48th Division.

1/8th BATTALION

WORCESTERSHIRE REGIMENT

SEPTEMBER 1 9 1 6

144th Brigade.

48th Division.

1/8th BATTALION

WORCESTERSHIRE REGIMENT

OCTOBER 1 9 1 6

144th Brigade.
48th Division.

1/8th BATTALION

WORCESTERSHIRE REGIMENT

NOVEMBER 1 9 1 6

144th Brigade.

48th Division.

1/8th BATTALION

WORCESTERSHIRE REGIMENT

DECEMBER 1 9 1 6

At zero hour, Box barrage
opens M.10.c.67 — 8065 — 98 —
M.10.d.95 — 8530 — M.11.c.02.

Howitzers on M.10.c.8065 and
M.10.c.98 and M.10.d.5065

Rate of fire 0.0 — 0.03 intense
fire. 0.03 — 0.30 about 2 rounds
per gun per minute — after
0.30 1 round per gun per minute.
At order all in all guns
will drop on to front line
with intense fire for five
minutes & then stop.

1/8th. Bn. The Worcestershire Regt.   APPENDIX A

Operations of the 9th October 1917.
Ref. Map POELCAPPELLE 1:10000.

The battalion was in Brigade Reserve to an attack made by the remainder of the Brigade as follows:

Left	Centre	Right
1/4 GLOUCESTERS.	1/6 GLOUCESTERS	1/7 WORCESTERS

Objectives were as follows:

	Left	Centre	Right
1.	OXFORD Ho. and Adjacent Gunpits.	BURNS Ho and VACHER FM.	ADLER FM. and INCH Ho.
2.	OXFORD Ho. SHAFT and BERKS Ho.	Conform to flanks.	WALLEMOLEN and VARLET FM.

Our front line ran TERRIER FM, COUNTY CROSS-ROADS hence along W edge of CEMETRY enclosure to D2d39 - D3c28.
Forming-up line V26 a 43 to D3c 00.

At 9.50 p.m. 8th Oct head of the battalion passed 2a Bridge. CANAL BANK and marched up ALBERTA track to ADMIRALS RD from hence MOUSETRAP TRACK was used. Head of the battalion reached SPRINGFIELD 12.10 a.m. 9th Oct and took up a position in VANCOUVER SPRINGFIELD - ARBRE area and dug in and rested. Bn. was reported all in and dug in under cover at 1.35 a.m. Bn. HQrs established at SPRINGFIELD.

At zero + 1 hour battalion started to move up to position N of STROOMBEEK behind WINCHESTER SPUR. At 7.35 a.m. all companies had reported in position & dug in. Zero was at 5.20 a.m.

The position taken up is as shown on attached map. The enemy barraged the STROOMBEEK heavily. The first three companies got into position without casualties but the last company (B. Coy.) lost 1 killed + about 20 wounded. All movement

1/8th Bn. The Worcestershire Regt.

was along HÜBNER TRACK, platoons at 50 yards distance and companies at 200 yards.

At 6.20 a.m. advanced Bn. HQrs, consisting of Lt. WATSON, 3 signallers and runners was established at YORK FARM. As soon as positions behind WINCHESTER had been taken up companies sent out parties to get in touch with line battalions and liaison was established as follows:

D Coy with 1/4 GLOUC.
C "   " 1/6 "
B "   " 1/7 WORCS.

Communication with Bn. HQrs maintained by runners. One or two visual messages were got through, but visual was not satisfactory as both sending-station at YORK FM. and transmitting at ARBRE were constantly obscured by bursting shells. Communication by runner proved to be satisfactory as they were able to move with great speed along the track. Communication with Brigade was by telephone.

At 6 a.m. C.O. reported to Brigade HQrs at ARTILLERY HOUSE, ST. JULIEN, acting under instructions of Brigadier.

At 7.5 a.m. orders were received to send 1 Coy to support of 1/4 GLOUC. Orders were accordingly sent to D Coy to move forward and attack, capture & consolidate OXFORD HOUSES. At the same time A Coy was ordered to keep in close touch with D Coy and to move at once on SHAFT if OXFORD Ho were taken. D Coy. then advanced to V 26 c 88 and halted. Patrols were sent forward to clear up the situation and find out where 1/4 Glouc. front line was. Owing to enemy rifle and machine gun fire these patrols failed, suffering several casualties including an officer and a sergeant wounded. Enemy fire came mainly from about V 26 d 59. The whole of the right area of the 1/4 GLOUC. seemed to be

3.   1/8th Bn. The Worcestershire Regt.

actively occupied by the enemy, but there was not much rifle fire from direction of the LEKKERBOTTERBEEK. O.C. D Coy reported that he did not consider that an ordinary attack on OXFORD HO. was practicable by day without artillery. Orders were then sent to O.C. D Coy to send forward "stalking" patrols of about 6 men each, moving from shell-hole to shell-hole, to get in touch with the enemy and use rifle grenades if possible. This was also attempted but owing to enemy rifle-fire did not meet with success.

At 11.30 a.m. I received orders to send one Coy to support 7th WORCS. in attack on ADLER FM. and INCH HO. O.C. B Coy was ordered to get into touch with advanced Bn. Hqrs. 1/7 Worcs. & get instructions from there. About 2 p.m. he received orders from 1/7 WORCS. to attack INCH HO. as soon as possible without artillery support. A conference of platoon commanders was held and preliminary orders issued fixing Zero at 5 p.m. At 2.45 p.m. B Coy moved to jumping off place along continuation of COUNTY CROSS ROADS VACHER FM, ADLER FM road about D3 a 43 – D3 a 15. During advance from STROOMBEEK the company came under heavy rifle & machine-gun fire, but only lost 1 man wounded. Orders were then given to attack at 5 p.m. and arrangements made with 1/7 WORCS for supporting fire on the flanks. At 4.45 p.m. our "heavies" opened fire on line of trees 300x in front of jumping-off place. As no artillery support had been arranged, O.C. Coy postponed attack till 5.30 p.m. The shelling continued and at 6.30 p.m. orders were received not to attack but to consolidate a front & support line. This was done, touch was gained with 7th WORCS. on both flanks and posts established at D3 a 26 and D3 a 35. At 2.10 p.m. orders

4.

were received from Brigade to place two companies at the disposal of the 1/4" GLOUC. for an attack on OXFORD HO. A & D Coys were detailed for this and at 4 p.m. O.C. A & D reported to Hqrs. 1/4 GLOUC. At 5 p.m. D Coy formed up on COUNTY CROSS ROADS under our barrage.

Formation:- Astride the QUEBEC - OXFORD HO. RD. two platoons in front line, two in support. At 4.40 p.m. A Coy advanced from their position on the STROOMBEEK VALLEY. in order to follow directly after D Coy when they went forward at 5.10 p.m. As soon as the leading two platoons had advanced 70 yards they came under rifle fire from both flanks and M.G. fire from the right and from MEBU and succeeded in silencing it and a slight further advance was made possible. Then of the two officers with the company, one was wounded and the other killed. The advance was continued until enemy fire became so rapid that a halt was made. Casualties had been heavy in the two leading platoons so the two platoon sergeants discussed the situation and decided that they could take the Mebu with covering fire from supports. A Corporal and a sergeant & two runners were sent off separately to communicate with support Coy. but each became a casualty before reaching them. An act of great gallantry was performed by Pte. CHESTERFIELD who crawled with a bomb in his hand to within 3 yards of Mebu. before being shot dead. The enemy then left their position and ran back; Then however they saw that our men were unable to advance owing to fire from flanks they returned. During this time our men fired on those of the enemy who were visible. When the enemy developed an attack from both flanks and as our men were in danger of being surrounded the two sergeants decided to withdraw to our original line. It had become quite impossible to take OXFORD HOUSES that night; only a few of the rifles would fire and they were outnumbered two to one, and actually being fired on from the rear & on the right.

The support (A) Coy had moved up at 4.40 pm to follow up, but in the confusion direction was slightly lost & in gaining it again, SHAFT was mistaken for OXFORD HOUSES. A position was taken up on left of CEMETRY and advance commenced. The Company came under enfilade M.G. fire from right & left.

Touch was lost with D Coy, but O.C. A Coy presumed that they must be in front and did not use rifle fire. The actual positions of Support & attacking companies must have been as shown on attached map at 5.30 pm.

Company was halted & patrols sent forward to find attacking company. They failed and O.C. A Coy then decided that he was lost, and to take up position in original front line and reorganise. This was done. These two companies where then withdrawn & relieved by "C" Coy who had not been in action. I consider that though this attack was a failure, all concerned great credit, both from a point of view of actually getting over the ground and for finding their way by maps.

Copy of Narrative by Major J. P. Bate M.C. who was at the time commanding this Bn.

APPENDIX B

Copy No. 11.

1/8th Bn. The Worcestershire Regt.
Operation Order No. 10.

Ref Map 36 c. S.W. 1/20,000.   14·X·17.

1. The Battalion will relieve the 24th Infantry Battalion of the 6th Canadian Infantry Brigade in the CHAUDIERE Left Sector tonight.

2. Battalion Headquarters and the two front Companies will parade at 3 p.m. and will entrain at W.30 d (Sheet 36 B) S.W. of VILLERS-AU-BOIS at 4 p.m.
   The two rear Companies will parade at 4.45 p.m. and entrain at the same place at 5.45 p.m.

3. "A" Company will relieve "D" Company in Right front trenches T.10 c and a.
   "C" Company will relieve "C" Company in Left front trenches T.10.a. and T.9.b.
   "B" Company will relieve "B" Company in Right Support trenches in T.20 b and a.
   "D" Company will relieve "A" Company in Left Support trenches in T.14.c. and T.15.a.

4. 31st Canadian Infantry Battalion has arranged for 5 guides to take Battalion to T.19.b.64, where guides for the 24th Battalion will meet Battalion as follows, at 6.15. p.m.
   1 per Platoon.
   1 " Company H.Q.
   2 for Battalion H.Q.
   1 " M.O.

5. Advanced Party, consisting of the Battalion Intelligence Officer and one Officer from each of "A" and "C" Companies, will proceed to the line this morning, and will be met by a guide at the W. end of HUMBER track at S.28 d.48 at 10.30 a.m.

6. The 24th Canadian Battalion will leave their Intelligence Officer and one Officer of each of the front Companies in the line until dawn on the 18th.

7. The Lewis Guns will be taken in on G.S. Limbered Wagons as follows:-
   'A' and 'C' Companies to T.15 b 55.
   'B' and 'D'   "   " T.20 b 34.
   Guides for the L.G. Sections will meet Platoons as follows:-
   'A' and 'C' Companies at T.15. a. 48.
   'B' " 'D'   "   "   T.14.c. 90.

8. Code word for reporting Relief complete will be VENN.

Issued at 10.30 a.m.

E. Gillett
Capt & Adjt.
1/8th Bn. The Worcestershire Regt.

Copies 1 to 3 retained.
       4 to 7 Companies.
       8. Q.M.
       9. T.O.
      10. R.S.M.

APPENDIX C

Copy No. 11.

1/8th Bn. The Worcestershire Regt.

Operation Order No. 11.   21·X·17

The Battalion will be relieved by two Companies of the 1/6th GLOUCESTERS in the Front line and by 1/7th WORCESTERS in the Support lines on the night of Oct 21/22 1917.

Guides. From the Front Companies:-
    1 for Company H.Q.   1 Per Platoon.
will be at Junction of PEGGIE and TEDDIE GERRARD at 6.30 p.m.
Disposition of Gloucester 2 Companies will be
    "D" Company on Right Front - "C" on Left Front.

Guides. From Support Companies:-
    1 for Company H.Q.   1 Per Platoon.
will be where the RED TRAIL joins PEGGIE TRENCH at 6.15 p.m.
Two guides for Companies will be on Main LENS-ARRAS Road: end of RED TRAIL at 5.30 p.m.

Transport. Lewis Gun Limbers will be at (one Forward Dump, one Rear Dump.) Guns will be put in boxes and loaded by Teams as they are relieved.

Company Mess Kits will go on their Limber.

All Petrol Tins will be brought to Dumps on relief, also <u>Rum Jars and Ration Bags.</u>

Company Commanders horses will be on Road at end of RED TRAIL on LENS-ARRAS Road.

On Relief Companies will march back to NEUVILLE-ST-VAAST by way of PEGGIE TRENCH, RED TRAIL to LENS-ARRAS Road, turn left along Main road to Cross Roads at 'LES TILLEULS' where Guides will direct. Guides for Platoons will be at CEMETERY Junction at entrance to NEUVILLE-ST-VAAST.

Company Commanders should see that each Platoon has a guide who knows the Red Trail.

Relief complete will be sent by Company Commanders NAME.

Gilbert
Capt & Adjt.
1/8th Bn. The Worcestershire Regt.

Copies:- 1 to 3 retained.
4 to 7 Companies.
8 R.S.M.
9. 1/7 Worcesters.
10. 1/6 Gloucesters.
11. War Diary.

APPENDIX D

Copy No. 3.

8th Bn. The Worcestershire Regt.
Operation Order No. 12.   25.X.17.

The Battalion will relieve the 9th Battn. The Worcestershire Regt. in Support on night of 25/26 October 1917, as under:—

"A" and "C" Companies will relieve the two Companies of the 9th Bn. The Worcestershire Regt. in CANADA and GERTIE Trench.

"B" Company will relieve the Company of the 9th Worcesters in VIMY.

"D" Company will relieve the Company of the 9th Worcesters in the BRICKFIELDS.

"C" Company will move from CELLAR CAMP at 5.15. p.m.
"A"   "   "   "   "   "   "   at 5.25. "
Headqrs "   "   "   "   "   "   at 5.35. "
"D" Company "   "   "   "   "   "   at 5.40. "
"B"   "   "   "   "   "   "   at 5.50. "

VIMY RIDGE will not be crossed till after dark.
In crossing the Ridge Humber Trench will <u>not</u> be used, Companies will go by the Road.

<u>Transport.</u>
1 Limber for "A" and "C" Companies for Lewis Guns and Officers' Mess Kits.
1 Half Limber for "B" Coy for Lewis Guns and Officers Mess Kits.
1 Half Limber for "D" (as above).
Mess Cart for Headqrs.
Transport will be at CELLAR CAMP at 4.30 p.m. and will move in rear of Companies.

Relief complete will be sent to Battn. Headqrs by name of Company Commander.

Battalion H.Q. will be at:—
ZOLLERN HOUSE
S.24.c.20.96.

(Signed) E. GILBERT.
Capt & Adjt.
8th Bn. The Worcestershire Regt.

Issued at 12.30 p.m.
Copies 1 to 3 retained.
   4 to 7 Companies.
   8. Q.M.
   9. T.O.
   10. R.S.M.
   11. 9 Worcesters.

APPENDIX E

Copy No. 13.

1/8th Bn. The Worcestershire Regt.
Operation Order No. 13.   29.10.17.

1. The Battalion will relieve the 1/7th Bn. The Worcestershire Regt. in the front line tonight, as follows:-
   'A' Coy will relieve 'A' Coy (Right Coy).
   'B' "   "   "   'B' " (Right Centre).
   'C' "   "   "   'C' " (Left Centre).
   'D' "   "   "   'D' " (Left Coy).

2. Guides of 1/7th Worc. Regt. for 'C' and 'D' Companies will be at junction of DORIS and HAYTER Trenches at 6 p.m.

3. Order of Move:-
   'D' starting at 5.30 p.m. followed by 'C' and Battn. H.Q.
   'B'   "   " 5.30 p.m.   "   " 'A'.

4. Relief complete to be wired by name of O.C. Company.

5. The 1/4th Gloucester Regt. will take over the present positions of Companies as follows:-
   'D' Company takes over from 'A'.
   'B'   "   "   "   " 'B'.
   'A'   "   "   "   " 'C'.
   'C'   "   "   "   " 'D'.

6. Guides for 1/4th Gloucester Regt. will be found by 'A' and 'C' Companies as follows:-
   1 for Company H.Q. and 1 per Platoon, at junction of RED TRAIL and LENS-ARRAS road, at 6.30 p.m.
   'D' Company will provide one guide at BRICKFIELDS at 6 p.m. to guide party to VICTORIA DUMP, to relieve our N.C.O. and 12 men.

            [signature]
            Capt & Adjt.
            1/8th Bn. The Worcestershire Regt.

Copies:- 1 to 3 retained.
         4 to 7 Companies.
         8 1/7th Worcesters.
         9 1/4th Gloucesters.
        10 Q.M.
        11 T.O.
        12 R.S.M.
        13 War Diary.

48TH DIVISION
144TH INFY BDE

144TH MACHINE GUN COY

JAN 1916 – ~~FEB 1918~~

1917 OCT

TO ITALY

144th Brigade.
48th Division.

144th BRIGADE MACHINE GUN COMPANY

JANUARY 1 9 1 6

Feb '18

144th Brigade.

48th Division.

144th BRIGADE MACHINE GUN COMPANY

FEBRUARY 1 9 1 6

Confidential

War Diary

of

Machine Gun Company
144th Infantry Brigade

from 1st February 1916 to 29th February 1916

(Volume 2)

144th Brigade.

48th Division.

144th BRIGADE MACHINE GUN COMPANY

MARCH 1 9 1 6

144th Brigade
48th Division.

144th BRIGADE MACHINE GUN COMPANY

APRIL 1 9 1 6

144th Brigade.
48th Division.

144th BRIGADE MACHINE GUN COMPANY

MAY 1916

144th Brigade.
48th Division.

144th BRIGADE MACHINE GUN COMPANY

JUNE 1916

144th Inf.Bde.
48th Div.

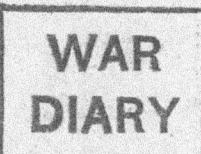

144th MACHINE GUN COMPANY.

J U L Y

1 9 1 6

Attached:
Appendices I, II & III.

APPENDICES

I
II
III

Appendices to War Diary July 1916.

Machine Gun Company, 144th Infantry Brigade.

APPENDIX II

OVILLERS 1916 July 16/17

1/4th Gloucester Regt. attacked Enemy trench from PT 99 Southwards to northern most point held by 1/7th Worcester Regt in OVILLERS

M Gs of A & B Section supported this attack, with covering & flanking fire. Six guns were used. 4 under 2/Lt Bond in positions in CONNISTON STREET & 2 under Lt DURANT in positions in DORSET STREET. OC attacking party spoke very highly of effect & support given to him by this fire — especially to his left flank.

No 1939 Corp. RENDLE did extremely good work & showed great initiative & resource in handling his two guns.

—"—

APPENDIX III

OVILLERS 22/23

1/6 Btn Gloucester Regt. attacked Pt redoubt Pt 90-40

M/Gs of B & D Sections supported this attack — by sweeping all ground in X2A & X2B (as far west as line joining PT 68. 55. 62. Communication trenches in this area were also continually searched & also communication trench from PT 78 - PT 74. Two guns were ready to move forward from PT 44. if attack was successful.

Though there was a continuous & intense bombardment. All guns were maintained in action & between 8000 & 9000 rounds were fired.

No 21761 Sgt Beavis — No 21760 Corp. Waldron showed great gallantry. At their own request they were No 1 on their guns & though the gun positions were repeatedly hit they never left their guns in action & refused to be relieved.

No 21092. Pte Hawkes — No 21095. Pte Newman also showed great coolness & devotion to duty & maintained their guns in action though they themselves were buried by shell fire.

A F Stubs Lieut & A/Capt
for O.C. Coy
No 144 M.G. Corps

144th Brigade
48th Division.

144th BRIGADE MACHINE GUN COMPANY

AUGUST 1 9 1 6

144th Brigade.
48th Division.

144th BRIGADE MACHINE GUN COMPANY

SEPTEMBER 1916

144th Brigade.

48th Division.

144th BRIGADE MACHINE GUN COMPANY

OCTOBER 1 9 1 6

144th Brigade.

48th Division.

144th BRIGADE MACHINE GUN COMPANY

NOVEMBER 1 9 1 6

144th Brigade.

48th Division.

144th BRIGADE MACHINE GUN COMPANY

DECEMBER 1 9 1 6

62c N.E. 1/20000

APPENDIX A
to WAR DIARY   APRIL 1917

Operations during period 1st April to 13th April 1917

(1)
a. It was decided to have 3 pairs of guns actually in action during the advance ie. 1 pair of three Sections with the remaining pair of each Section in Support. The fourth Section being in reserve.

b. The three main lines of advance were decided on :—
     a Along spur in F 25, 26 & 20
     b   "   "   in F 13, 19, & 14.
     c High ground round SAULCOURT to high ground in E 12, F 1 & 7, 2 & 8

c. The objectives being the line EPEHY, LEMPIRE & RONSSOY.

d. Transport of forward guns was kept well up & pack animals used extensively.

e. Each pair of guns always moved complete (ie. no dumps of any sort left behind) and with transport.

(2) ATTACK on EPEHY 5.30 am 1st April

Before operations commenced guns were disposed :—
2 guns under 2/Lt FOSTER. E side of ST EMILIE.
2 guns under Lt. JENNINGS E side of SAULCOURT.
D Section under 2/Lt BROWN Reserve.
Remaining (C) Section was in position just W of spur F 25 Central.

The following dispositions were made for the attack :—
① After dark 2/Lt FOSTER moved his guns to a position on railway about E 13 Central for flanking fire.
② D Section was brought up to SAULCOURT & also two Support teams of A Section.
    a Forward positions were prepared on each flank of Bde frontage and forward of line from which infantry were to start. Roughly :—
       1 pair just East of CAPRON COPSE for harassing fire against trenches in E 12 b, F 7 a.
       1 pair on southern edge of spur in E 11 d for covering fire on W edge of EPEHY
    These positions were occupied by pairs of guns from D & A Sections about 5 am.
    b Support guns of each Section moved behind infantry & approx objectives for consolidation given were :—
       1 High ground in F 7 a
       2 just forward of Eastern edge of village in F 1 d.

Attack was a complete success & four guns consolidated & reached objectives after operations ~~taken from guns~~ in position for covering fire were withdrawn & guns under 2/Lt FOSTER moved along spur to F.19 b.99

3. **FLANK ATTACK** to 145 Inf Bde's attack on RONSSOY, LEMPIRE & BASSE-BOULOGNE made by 8th Worcesters 5am 5th April.

Attack was made as defensive flank against "chalk cliffs" in F.27 & Spur in F.28.

Preparatory to attack B Section under 2/Lt PEMBERTON & 2/Lt. FOSTER were in positions on high ground in F.26.a for covering fire :—

Objectives for consolidation
        a. One pair chalk cliffs in F.27.
        b. " " Spur in F.28.

Covering fire could not be given owing to darkness & uncertainty of position of our troops, but objectives for consolidation were gained.

4. **ATTACK on ridge from F.29.b – F.17.b.** 13th April 4 am.

Only Co-operation possible was flanking fire from Spur in F.6.c.rd against SART FM & vicinity. This was done & it was thought to have been effective.

H. H. Field
Capt & OC
144 M.G Coy.

144. MACHINE GUN COMPANY.

List of Casualties for the month of August 1917

KILLED.

No. 54759	Pte.	Crook C.	M.G.C.	14-8-17
	2nd. Lieut.	G.Mackay.	Mdlsx. Regt.	16-8-17
70822	Pte.	Taylor H.	M.G.C.	"
No. 55882	"	Clack J.	"	"
No. 67898	"	Ramsey H.	"	"
No. 66304	"	Hullah J.	"	"
No. 241879	"	Jauncey W.	1/8th. Worcs.	"
No. 34223	"	Smith E.	1/7th. Worcs.	"
No. 203107	"	Woolley E.W.	" "	"
No. 73596	"	Fowler E.A.	M.G.C.	19-8-17
No. 10088	"	Barrett T.	"	"
No. 57334	"	Edwards A.	"	"
No. 70615	"	Whittle J.	"	"
No. 73597	"	Jeffrey T.	"	"
No. 240340	"	Chance C.	1/8th. Worcs.	22-8-17

DIED OF WOUNDS.

No. 22297	L/Cpl.	Strawbridge	M.G.C.	13-8-17
No. 22556	"	Richards H.	"	23-8-17
No. 58396	Pte.	Comery H.	"	25-8-17

MISSING.

No. 202326	Pte.	Poffley G.W.	1/7th. Worcs	16-8-17

WOUNDED.

No. 14913	Pte.	Malin F.	M.G.C.	7-8-17
No. 22297	L/Cpl.	Strawbridge	"	9-8-17
No. 24584	Pte.	Lodge E.G.	1/4th. Glos.	8-8-17
No. 72995	Sergt.	Tombs A.	M.G.C.	16-8-17
No. 32566	Cpl.	Tolley T.	"	"
No. 21095	L/Cpl	Newman W.	"	"
No. 22563	"	Crisp A.	"	"
No. 22556	"	Richards H.	"	"
No. 42001	Pte.	Foster W.	"	"
No. 31595	"	Rosendale F.	"	"
No. 58396	"	Comery H.	"	"
No. 200315	"	Broome E.H.	1/7th. Worcs.	"
No. 202117	"	Evans H.	" "	"
No. 36219	"	Rollings H.	" "	"
No. 202197	"	Barton J.	" "	"
No. 242429	"	Sherman C.	1/8th. Worcs.	"
bNo. 26637	"	Hamblin A.	1/6th Glos.	19-8-17
No. 72932	Sergt.	Bolt.C.	M.G.C.	"
No. 21077	L/Cpl.	Postins A	"	"
No. 57108	Pte.	Chambers B.	"	"
No. 45253	"	Coughlan J.	"	"
No. 32290	"	French H.B.	"	"
No. 70599	"	Larcombe W.C.	"	"
No. 57125	"	Cribb T.	"	"
No. 42018	"	Jeffrey A.L.	"	22-8-17
No. 6507	"	Cannon J.	"	"
No. 92309	"	Reid J.	"	"
No. 300999	"	Wheeler W.	1/4th. Glos.	27-8-17

List of Casualties, cont.

WOUNDED (GASSED)

No. 56865	Pte.	Allcorn	M.G.C.	9-8-17
No. 57438	"	Barker S.	"	"
No. 70603	"	Coventry W.	"	"
No. 56449	"	Crook H.	"	"
No. 88165	"	Dewhurst G.	"	"
No. 54794	"	Evans D.E.	"	"
No. 267136	"	Jackson D.E.	"	"
No. 20190	"	Keatings	1/6th. Glos.	"
No. 21382	"	Mitten F.J.	" "	"
No. 267136	"	Harman J.	" "	"
No. 28495	"	Dale P.	" "	"
No. 267400	"	Whittaker A.	" "	"
No. 266418	"	Bohin E.	" "	"
~~NxyxxPRWMx~~				
No. 2027	"	Edwards F.	" "	"
No. 21087	"	Lacey H.	M.G.C.	14-8-17
No. 70610	"	Westwood R.	"	"
No. 53687	"	Thomson G.	"	"

144. MACHINE GUN COMPANY.

Report on operations :-
4th. October, and 9th. & 10th. October, 1917.

(1) The Company, assisted by two sections of 194th. M.G.Coy. co-operated with 143rd. Infantry Brigade in their attack on the line TWEED HO. WINCHESTER FARM", WELLINGTON, by firing a barrage. (Map showing zero lines, approximate positions, and lifts, attached.

Points brought out.

RECONNAISANCE AND DIGGING IN.

There was only one area from which the barrage could be fired and this was very carefully reconnoitred for three days. Fortunately, enemy shelled area on each of these days and an accurate idea of barrage lines was thus formed. The value of this reconnaisance cannot be too much enforced, as though area was heavily shelled the whole time, batteries escaped full force of barrage and as they had dug in, many casualties were saved. Head cover for gun positions made from "Baby Elephant" shelters were invaluable against splinters.

LENGTH OF BARRAGE.

Distance between guns, 10 yards, between half batteries, 30 yards.

EXPENDITURE OF AMMUNITION.

Batteries had to fire for 4 hours 52 minutes, and be prepared for S.O.S. at the end. This necessitated a very large amount of S.A.A. which had to be man-hauled for over 1500 yards.

The strain on the men caused by these carrying parties was very great, and caused many casualties from sickness alone, chiefly overstrain.

A pool of belt boxes in "Active Corps" would be extremely valuable for barrages.

" T " pieces were found to be invaluable.

- 2 -

Aiming Posts.

These cannot be relied on and it must be impressed on all ranks that an A.A.M. on the ground which is not likely to be altered by shell fire must be chosen for each gun, as aiming posts were being continually destroyed.

Personnel.

Batteries of 8 guns, sub-divided into half batteries of 4 guns.

Half battery consisting of :-

    1 Officer.
    1 Sergeant.
    4 men per gun.

COMMUNICATION.

Runner and Visual.

Visual difficult owing to misty weather, would have been far easier if LUCAS LAMPS had been available, and I consider that at least 4 of these, if not 5, should be on the establishment of a M.G.Coy. during Active operations.

ADVANCE TO 2nd. POSITION.

Not attempted owing to condition of ground, and not advised unless absolutely necessary.

The Company withdrew in the Early afternoon under orders from Division.

CASUALTIES.

Killed 2 O.R.   Wounded 5 O.R.   Wounded at Duty 2 O.R.
2 Guns.   (4-10-17)

The barrage entails great strain on the personnel especially when "original lines" with good system of communication" have been left, and when ample time is not given to the Company allotted the task, - and in my opinion, no Company should be detailed for this work when the Brigade to which it belongs is due for an attack. In the case in question the Company was employed for 2 days previous to barrage, in carrying S.A.A. etc., and had most of the "Edge" taken off it by the time the Brigade attacked on the 9th. inst.

A report on the operations of the 9th.,10th.inst.is attached.

Supplementary points of interest.

Formation for an attack with two objectives.

Sections working in depth, each sub-section moving close

- 3 -

behind infantry detailed for thecapture of approximate objectives allotted to that sub-section for consolidation.

Officer with orderlies in advance of sub-section for reconnaisance, and for keeping in touch with situation.

The following to be impressed on all ranks :-

(1) Approximate objective.
(2) To bear in mind that assistance must be given to infantry whenever possible
(3) Position of forward dump of belt boxes.

Section or Sections in reserve in a central position.

N.B. They should move to their position (which must be reconnoitred) before Zero and dig in, and it is of the utmost importance that good communication is kept with them. They should be used for filling gaps caused by casualties or exposed flanks or with reserves used to exploit sucess beyond original objective.

In my opinion more casualties are caused by enemy barrage falling on forming up positions and back areas, shortly after Zero if Sections wait until situation is clear before moving forward than by M.Gun and rifle fire if they move in close support of infantry. Another advantage of the latter procedure being that assistance can often be given to infantry during advance.

Personnel.   Sub-sections.

Officer's Orderly.
Responsible N.C.O.
Teams of 4 M.Gunners and 2 carriers

A proportion of M.Gunners in reserve if possible & also a party of carriers.

AMMUNITION SUPPLY.
8 boxes per gun to be carried forward by each team. More than 2 boxes per man is too much and more than 6 men per team too many to control satisfactorily.

Spare carriers to be used to carry from a forward dump of belt boxes made before Zero in front line to central position in 1st. Objective.

CASUALTIES.   Killed 1 Officer, 6 O.R.   Wounded 10 O.R.
              Missing 1 O.R.   (9/10-10-17).

---------------oo0oo---------------

144 MACHINE GUN COMPANY.

Report on operations 9th. and 10th. October 1917.

(1) Orders for move to the line were received at 1-15 p.m. on the 8th. inst. at REIGERSBURG CAMP, and it was decided to move to preliminary positions, JANET FARM, and the TRIANGLE Area as soon as possible in order to give the troops a rest there, and a hot meal before moving into forming up positions. The Company therefore moved off between 3-30 and 3-45 p.m. and were in positions mentioned above about 7-15 p.m. Owing to the weather- condition of the ground etc. it was found impossible to give the men a hot meal and the value of the rest was greatly decreased owing to heavy rain.

(2) DISPOSITIONS ETC.

Owing to 2 guns being rendered useless by shell fire during the operations 4th. October, only 14 guns were employed and orders were issued as follows :-

(Sub-section) C Section to co-operate with 1/7th Worcester Btn. with approximate objectives for consolidation
    a. Sub-section ADLER FARM.
    b. " " Strong point S. of VARLET FARM

A Section to co-operate with 1/6th. Glos. Regt. with approximate objective for consolidation
    BURNS HO.

B Section to co-operate with 1/4th. Glos. Regt. with approximate objectives for consolidation
    a. Strong point N.E. of OXFORD HO.(Sub-section)
    b. Between SHAFT and BERKS Hos. (Sub-section)

D Section In reserve near YORK FARM.

Coy. H.Q. Pill box next to ARTILLERY HO.

Report Centres H.Q. 1/7th. Btn. Worcester Regt. and HUBNER.

Communication. Relay runner posts.

Sub-sections were to go over behind the last wave of infantry detailed to capture approximate objectives allotted to sub-section.

(3)   C Section (with 1/7th. Worcester Regt.) were in position behind waves ¼ hour before Zero, but shortly after Zero, sub-section detailed for ADLER FARM was wiped out by shell fire and guns destroyed. Officer I/C this sub-section reported this to other sub-section Officer who moved into his place. During advance this sub-section followed in close support of infantry and in communication with Company Officer. As situation remained obscure at ADLER FARM, officer sent message back to Battalion Forward H.Q. and at their request consolidated "SUPPORT LINE"

O.C. 1/7th. Btn. Worcester Regt. reported on the able and determined conduct of LT. RAYNER and 2nd. LT. MILLAR, and the assistance given to the infantry by this section.

A Section. (sub-section) with 1/6th. Glos. Regt. was in position one hour before Zero and advanced in close support of Infantry. Just before reaching BURNS HOUSE, Officer in charge was killed and one gun and most of team put out of action, but Corporal I/C took up position just behind BURNS HOUSE.

B Section with 1/4th. Glos. Regt. moved from preliminary position to HUBNER and picked up guide for TWEED HOUSE. This guide and two others lost Section and it was unable to get to forming up positions before Zero. Close touch was eventually kept with Battalion H.Q. and a sub-section (the other two guns having been knocked out) took up positions near TWEED HOUSE. The Officer I/C of this Section reconnoitred forward and could find no better positions and could not reach OXFORD HOUSES.

Various targets (snipers and M/guns) were engaged.

D. Section remained in reserve and were not used.

(4) Our barrage was reported to be weak and patchy as compared to that on the 4th. inst.

(5) Observation Posts used were :-
ARBRE", HUBNER, VICTORIA HOUSE.

(6) Guns were kept in action despite the mud as canvas covers were used in all cases, but belt boxes were much affected by wet and mud.

- 3 -

(7) <u>Covering Fire</u>   was given by 145 M.G.Coy.

(8) <u>Missing</u>   2 O.R., but not believed to be prisoners.

(9) <u>Wounded</u>   were evacuated.

                                        Captain,
                              Cmmdg., 144. Machine Gun Company.

INTELLIGENCE SUMMARY.
(Erase heading not required.)

Summaries are contained in F.S. Regs., Part II. and the Staff Manual respectively. Title pages will be prepared in manuscript.

Place	Date 1916	Hour	Summary of Events and Information	Remarks and references to Appendices
	February			
	20		Draft of 95 O.R. from Base. Working parties & platoons from HANNESCAMPS	
			joined Battalion in BIENVILLERS.	
	21		G.O.C. Brigade inspected billets in morning behind 8th Bn Worcester Regt	
			in "D" Section.	
	22		Some snow in morning. G.O.C. Bde visited Battalion HQrs, and the left	
			two Companies	
	23		Trenches – Quiet day – keen frost at night	
	24		" Quiet day – snow, still very cold	rest?
	25		" Fine snow all morning. G.O.C. Bde went round left	
			half Battalion Line with Capt. BENNETT. Relieved by 8th Worcester Regt	
			All in Billets SOUASTRE by 11·0 p.m.	
	26		More snow in the night. Large parties on road clearing under orders	
			of the Town Major.	
	27		Church parade 12 noon. G.O.C. Division present, and Deputy Chaplain	
			General took the Service. More snow and more parties road clearing	
	28		Thaw began. C.O. inspected billets. Lecture at 6·0 p.m. by G.S.O. III Divison	
			on Aeroplane photographs.	

WAR DIARY or INTELLIGENCE SUMMARY

Army Form C. 2118.

Place	Date	Hour	Summary of Events and Information	Remarks and references to Appendices
COURCELLES	March 20		Billets in Div. Curios performed in School of Instruction at 7.30pm. Divn. Corps	
	21.		Baths at SAILLY 9 am. to 5pm. Cinema 5 + 7 pm.	
	22.		Billets	
	23.		Relieved 9" Worcesters in trenches. Relief comp(l)eted about 9.30pm	
Trenches 57D.N.34	24.		Quiet. Snow	
	25.		Quiet. Snow.	
	26.		Quiet. Snow.	
	27.		Relieved by 9" Worcesters. Bn. proceeds to Winnizeele.	A.9.W.
COURCAMPS 57.N.R.25E	28.		Billets. Bn. Methuish attends demonstration at Divl. Anti Gas School. Working Parties.	
	29.		Billets. Working Park	
	30.		Major Tomkinson proceeds on leave + Capt Adam assumes command of Bn.	
	31.		Billets. Courcamps shelled during afternoon by 5.9" Shells. 2 on direct hit on church. 2 on Bn. Headquarters. R.G.A. West Riding Battery and R.E. H.6rs badly hit. R.G.A. + West Riding billets burnt to ground. About 100 shells during afternoon. Casualties about 9 men at Bde HQrs. 6 evacuated.	

H. Robson Capt.
Comdg. 7"/8m. The Worcestershire Regt.

INTELLIGENCE SUMMARY. 1/1 [illegible]

VOL 14

Place	Date	Hour	Summary of Events and Information	Remarks and references to Appendices
	1916 May			
COUIN	1	Trenches	Capt N.P. GOODWIN wounded in isolated post in Centre Company by Rifle Grenade. One man killed.	
	2	"	Relieved in Trenches by 4th Oxford & Bucks L.I. in the afternoon.	
	3	Hts to Billets	Bn moved to Huts at COUIN. Bn all found in Billets at 1.30 a.m. on 3rd inst.	
BEAUVAL	4		Bn prepares for march to BEAUVAL on following day. Reveille 2.30 a.m. Bn paraded at 4.40 a.m. March to BEAUVAL. Brigadier & Divl Gen, & Corps Commander all seemed to be pleased with the march and complimented the Brigade on it. Only 2 men in the Brigade fell out.	11.15
	5	"	Companies at disposal of O.C. Companies.	
	6	"	Company training on limited training grounds.	
	7	"	Brigade Church Parade at 11-0 a.m. Bn Band supplied the Music.	
	8	"	Company training. LIEUT. COL. A.R.HARMAN returns to the Battalion, but assumes temporary command of the Brigade in the absence of the Brigadier.	

Place	Date	Hour	Summary of Events and Information	Remarks and references to Appendices
Trenches	May 31 1916		Quiet day. Our 9·25 shewed the HOOK.	GHS

A. Farman Lieut. Col.
Comdg. 1/7th Bn Worcestershire Regt.

INTELLIGENCE SUMMARY.
(Erase heading not required.)

Place	Date 1916	Hour	Summary of Events and Information	Remarks and references to Appendices
W.8.d.	August 14.		Bn. in bivouac. Operations by 6th Gloucesters	
	15		do do do do	
	16.		Bde relieved by 143rd Inf Bde. Bn. to camp at V.12.c.	
V.12.c.	17		Bn. in camp.	
	18		Successful operations by 143rd Inf Bde. Bn. standing by in camp all day and night.	
X.3.c.6.8.	19		Bn. relieved 5th Bn. The Gloucestershire Regt in trenches – Relief complete 6·0 p.m. Area:– Right (1st Anzac div) at 57 D.R.33 a.81. along SKYLINE TR. to X.2.6.7.8. thence X.2.6.4.6 with advanced posts at 4.8. 6th R. Warwicks on our left. Quiet night.	
	20	12 noon	00.98 Bn. to side slip WEST. Following adjustments to take place – 2·0 pm 'A' Coy takes over 96-96-06 from 6th R.W.R. 'B' Coy still holds 46-46-62. SKYLINE TR. is taken over by from us by 7th R. War. R. 6th Glos. on our left. Bn. HQrs. moves to X.8.a.8.5.	
X.8.a.8.5.			Adjustment complete 4·30 p.m. 5·50 p.m. A.H.20.21 to B & A operations for tonight 'A' to bomb to 79. 'B' to find & hold 59. 6th Glos. attacking 19-29-27-34.	

INTELLIGENCE SUMMARY

(Erase heading not required.)

Place	Date	Hour	Summary of Events and Information	Remarks and references to Appendices
AUGUST 1916. X.8.a.8.5.	20th (contd)			
	21st	9-32 p.m.	From 6th Glos. we are at 19. 10-32 p.m. 30 Bde A.H. 26. Have good 59.	
		12-15 a.m.	6th Blrs at 19. 50x holding 19-29-27. 12-35 a.m. from O-C 'A' A.B. 6 "79 strongly held" Lt MELHUISH wounded. 1-20 a.m. 'A' Coy within 20x of 79. 6th Glos. trying to relieve pressure by attacking 31. 3-12 a.m. A.13.10 from O-C 'A' Am falling back to 76. 7-0 a.m. 'D' Coy returned to 'A' Coy. 10-35 a.m. A.H.H.2. Arranging further Artillery preparation of 79-91. 10-45 a.m. Rec'd O.O. no.99. 6th Glos. will attack 31. 7100 as 99-91. Zero Time 12 noon.	
		10-50 a.m.	A.H.H.3 to 'D' giving orders for 2 Platoons to attack 79-91. 10-55 a.m. A.H.H 4 to 'B' to move 20. 11-35 a.m. A.H. H.7 to 'C' to send 2 Sections to open up 59-99 and to get in touch with 'B' at 20. [Note there 2 Sections under 2/Lt BAXTER attked well under heavy shell fire digging from 59 to 99. By Evening 46-59-99 had been opened up.] 12-26 a.m. from O-C 'D' Coy 2 Platoons under Lt PEAKE advanced at 12-4 going well. 12-35 p.m. A.H. 48.15 O-C 'D' 6th Glos. report your men well in [note - the objective was invisible from any point on our line being on the reverse slope] to trench 76-79 passable. 1-10 p.m. from O-C 'D' Am reaching up more bombs Casualties 5 wounded. 1-20 p.m. from O-C 'B' 2 Sections under Lt. LLOYD who went up for 20 have disappeared. 1-25 p.m. from 6 Glos. failed to get 31. 1-28 p.m. O-C 'D' reports his assaulting platoons between 76 and 79. trying to bomb to 79. 1-30 a.m. 6th Glos. report they have 31. 2-6 p.m. A.H.53 O-C 'D' Coy. At 3-30/pm Sharpnel barrage on 91. Have 1 Platoon prepared to assault.	

INTELLIGENCE SUMMARY

(Erase heading not required.)

Instructions regarding War Diaries and Intelligence Summaries are contained in F.S. Regs., Part II. and the Staff Manual respectively. Title Pages will be prepared in manuscript.

Place	Date AUGUST 1916	Hour	Summary of Events and Information	Remarks and references to Appendices
X 2 a 6.5.	22nd cont.	4-40 p.m.	A.H. 79 to O.C. C Coy. Major T. Lve. visits your line and is of opinion that trench junction 27-79 is in rear of your bomb stop. Send daylight patrol up old trench to get touch with 6 Glos at 27. 5-H.J. from O.O. 102 cancelled. El is in our possession. 7-20 p.m. R.1.R. to No 103. 7 words. Re Glos to attack Zero time 10-30 a.m. 1st objective 29-79. 2nd objective 31-29. 8-30 p.m. From O.C. C Coy. patrols have found 6 & 2 Cor at 2-7. On leaving trench 76-79 they went over hill for about 50 yards and then hit good trench (27-99) leading to 6 Glos post. 9-27 p.m. Recd R.M. R.H.I. [Rele hit good trench will be relieved to-morrow by 145 Bde and by 25" Division. All operations for to-morrow cancelled.	
	23	3-0 a.m.	R.C.A. patrol reports on trench 79-31. Lieut CARTER, left the patrol C. 1-45 a.m. R.C.A. relief orders (B.O. No 104) 9-0 a.m. Bn. returned by H.Q. O.B.L.I. Relief complete 9-0 a.m. on relief Bn. to camp in V.12.C.	
V.12.C.	24		Bn. in camp Baths at BOUZINCOURT	
	25		do.	
	26		do.	
FORCEVILLE	27		Bn. moved to FORCEVILLE. All in huts by 5-0 p.m. C.O. & O.C. Coys. went on in morning to reconnoitre trench line.	
Q.9.q.3.	28.		Coys. moved out independently and concentrated at P.18.C. where men had dinner. Heavy rain. Coys. moved from line to relieve 1st BUFFS. Relief complete 2-0 p.m. Bn. H.Qrs. at Q.9.b.93. Area:- from Q.10.b.15.05. to Q.H.d.4.4. 6 & 2 Lvs on our right. 8th Worcs. on our left.	
	29	Night.	Rain began again. Otherwise very quiet.	
	30		Rain continued. Trenches facing in 'D' Coy moved back to cellars in AUCHONVILLERS.	
	31		Fine day. A little shelling by enemy. Our guns were cutting.	

A. F. Graham Lieut. Col.
Comdg. 1/7th Bn. Worcestershire Regt.

WAR DIARY
or
INTELLIGENCE SUMMARY

Army Form C. 2118.

Place	Date	Hour	Summary of Events and Information	Remarks and references to Appendices
HUPPY	January 8.		Arrived village at 2.30 am. Troops were billetted during arch heavy snowstorm. Transport arrived at 7 a.m. The transport which set out from BAIZIEUX early in the morning of the 7th arrived in HUPPY on the evening of the 8th, after a severe trying crossed to bits.	
	9.		Billets. — Coys were placed at the disposal of O.C. Coys for cleaning up of interior economy.	
	10.		A Bath Van with frequent snowstorms.	
	11, 12, 13.		Billets. 1 Coy trained under 1 Cov arrangements.	
			Billets. Coys at disposal of O.C. Coys for training in Digging, rapid wiring, bayonet fighting.	
	14.		Bombing. Cross order drills.	
	15.		Billets. Voluntary Church Service.	
	Feb 18, 19 3.		Coys at disposal of O.C. Coys for training in Bayonet fighting, digging, & rapid	
			wiring, musketry & coys attack.	
	20.		Battalion practised this attack.	
	21.		Billets. Church parade under Coy arrangement.	
	22 & 23rd		Billets. Bn. marched to MALLENCOURT and practised the attack as part of. Brigade.	
	24.		Coys at disposal of O.C. Coys for tactical exercises.	
	25.		Coys at disposal of O.C. Coys for interior economy.	
	26.		Monday A.T. 6.15 am. to move to new area. Coys at disposal of O.C. Coys	
			for tactical exercises. school work march.	
	27.		Coys at disposal of O.C. Coys for marching order inspection & route march.	

Army Form C. 2118.

WAR DIARY
or
INTELLIGENCE SUMMARY.
(Erase heading not required.)

Instructions regarding War Diaries and Intelligence Summaries are contained in F. S. Regs., Part II. and the Staff Manual respectively. Title pages will be prepared in manuscript.

Place	Date	Hour	Summary of Events and Information	Remarks and references to Appendices
CAPPY	1917 March 9.		A working party of 2 Offs & 125 O.R. was sent to MEREAUCOURT WOOD at H.20.6.22. A, B & D Coys to FROISSY for baths.	
do	10.		Working party of 2 Offs & 125 O.R. sent to H.20.6.22.	
do	11.		A & B Coys out on working parties in forward area.	
do	12.		A Court of Enquiry on the Billet fire of 11 Feb/17 was held at Batt. H.Q. Ranges at G.26.c. used by A & D Coys & Lewis gunners. Coys practice trench to trench attack.	
Support Trenches	13.		Move up to support line to relieve the 1/1 Bucks Batt. in ACHILLE RAVINE. Relief complete at 9.45 pm.	
do	14		Working parties found to clean the main C.T.s & to improve & construct dugouts.	
do	15		Working parties carry on with yesterday's work. 2 O.R.s wounded by shell fire	
do	16		Batt. received orders to provide working & carrying parties to assist the 145 Bde. who are to make an attack on LA MAISONETTE in the morning	

Army Form C. 2118.

WAR DIARY
or
INTELLIGENCE SUMMARY.
(Erase heading not required.)

Instructions regarding War Diaries and Intelligence Summaries are contained in F. S. Regs., Part II. and the Staff Manual respectively. Title pages will be prepared in manuscript.

Place	Date	Hour	Summary of Events and Information	Remarks and references to Appendices
LE MESNIL	1917 March 21	8 a.m.	The Batt'n is relieved by the 4 R Berkshire Reg't & marches back to its old billets in ACHILLE RAVINE.	
ACHILLE RAVINE	22		Two working parties of 100 men each found to work on LAMIRÉ FARM BRIDGE	
	23		Working parties found as follows:— 50 O.R. at LAMIRÉ FARM BRIDGE. 100 O.R. on BARLEUX - FLAUCOURT ROAD. 20 O.R. on SALVAGE WORK. Remainder sent for baths at HERBECOURT.	
	24		Working parties as yesterday.	
	25	10.40 a.m.	Working parties continued. Orders received to move to billets in PERONNE	
		2.30 p.m.	The Batt'n less working parties moves into PERONNE by the FAUB'G de PARIS entrance & takes up good billets in the ruins. The working parties follow on after completing their work.	

Army Form C. 2118.

WAR DIARY
or
INTELLIGENCE SUMMARY.
(Erase heading not required.)

Instructions regarding War Diaries and Intelligence Summaries are contained in F. S. Regs., Part II. and the Staff Manual respectively. Title pages will be prepared in manuscript.

Place	Date	Hour	Summary of Events and Information	Remarks and references to Appendices
POPERINGHE	1917 July 27		Coys at disposal of O/c. Coys	
	28		do	
	29		Voluntary Church Service. 60 shells in the Town. 2 O.R slightly wounded.	
	30		Route March 6.a.m - 8.a.m.	
	31		March to camp in A 29 d. at 8.a.m.	
			Casualties for the month	
			2. O.R. slightly wounded	

Thompson Lieut. Col.
Comdr. 1/7th Bn. Worcestershire Regt.

WAR DIARY
or
INTELLIGENCE SUMMARY.

(Erase heading not required.) 1/8th BATTN. THE WORCESTERSHIRE REGT.

Army Form C. 2118.

Place	Date	Hour	Summary of Events and Information	Remarks and references to Appendices
	1916 Mch 5 Cont.		great discomfort of all especially those occupying the front line posts where in many cases no shelter could be provided. The lines here were from 100 to 200 yds apart, the greater part of our line being in easy range of German rifle grenade range and too far away from the enemy's line for the shorter range of our rifle grenades; also the enemy had several large Minenwerfer and also used a large number of trench bombs whereas our smaller trench mortars were unable to fire owing to lack of ammunition, the personnel was not in fact taken out of the line to improve billets. These facts, together with the bad weather conditions had a very dispiriting effect upon the men in the trenches who had to remain and be hammered while they were unable to reply. Our line here was formed by 13 posts, 6 of which were isolated and could only be relieved at night across the open, the wire in front was very weak, and in front of the 3 centre posts there was no wire at all, this portion having been severely bombarded just before it was taken over by the Batt.	

Army Form C. 2118.

WAR DIARY
or
INTELLIGENCE SUMMARY.
(Erase heading not required.) 1/8th BATTN. THE WORCESTERSHIRE REGT

Place	Date	Hour	Summary of Events and Information	Remarks and references to Appendices
	1916 Mch 5 cont		when a minor attack was made by the enemy from the "QUADRILATERAL". Our support line here and the communication trenches were chiefly old German trenches captured by the French in their attack on SERRE in 1915.	
	6		2 Lt BELL J.C. 3rd Gordon Regt RF was attached to the Battn as acting officer.	
COLINCAMPS.	7.		The Battn evacuated the trenches and proceeded to COLINCAMPS being relieved by the 7th Worc Regt. This tour was spent in working on the Bde reserve line and trenches leading to it. The relief were lengthened to four days as it was found that two days in round was not long enough for the men to dry their clothes	
Trenches opposite SERRE	11		The 13th relieved the 7th Batt Worc Regt in the trenches as before, the 14th R.I.R being on the right and the 6th Glouc. on the left. 2 Lt R.S.MILLER joined the Batt. from the 3rd Divn.	
	12		2 Lt H.G.C.CARTER and 2 Lt H.H.G.BENNETT rejoined the Bn from 3rd Divn. The moon during this tour was very bright, making it very difficult to relieve the front line.	

INTELLIGENCE SUMMARY.
8th BATTN. THE WORCESTERSHIRE REGT.

Place	Date	Hour	Summary of Events and Information	Remarks and references to Appendices
BOUZINCOURT	1916		When the old German line was occupied by the R.B.s had been reconnoitred, & the Battn. was prepared to take over in the afternoon. (of 26th July) a digging party strength 18 Officers 520 O.R. working on a new Communication trench on the ALBERT - POZIERES road, was caught in a barrage of 5.9", 4.2", 77 mm shells. The damage done by these was slight, but they were only the lead part of the barrage, the major portion being gas shells of a type which we had not hitherto seen ourselves. They exploded with but slight noise — so slight as to be mistaken by many for "blinds." Consequently many men were late in putting on their field helmets, & have realised the danger early enough for the smell of the gas employed was a novelty to everyone. By the forward, 598 of O.R. would present only 18 were entirely unaffected. The barrage lasted from 11.10 p.m. — 1.45 a.m. Capt J.P. BATE, in command of the party handled the situation in a cool & skilful manner; as a result of this & of the able cooperation of the other officers present, the party continued as far as possible at work till 1.55 a.m. & returned to billets in excellent order. Casualties 7 Officers killed, 29 Officers 36 O.R. suffering from gas poison & others, most of whom were attended to at	

WO95/2759-3

144 Bde MG Coy

Jan 1916 - Oct 1917

WAR DIARY or INTELLIGENCE SUMMARY

Army Form C. 2118.

Machine Gun Company, 144th Infant. Brigade.

Place	Date	Hour	Summary of Events and Information	Remarks and references to Appendices
	1916 April			
SAILLY	27		N.C.O. sent to Divisional Gas School. No 2732 Pte Sandy 5 Th. Sept 17 3 men arrived and wt. field	
	29		L A.B. r C. Return	

WAR DIARY or INTELLIGENCE SUMMARY

Machine Gun Company.
144th Infantry Brigade.

(Erase heading not required.)

Place	Date	Hour	Summary of Events and Information	Remarks and references to Appendices
MARTINPUICH	1916			
	15	20.	B Section returned to Trenches opposite The BUTTE	} B Section relieved
	"		" " 143 M.G. Coy in Trenches opposite LESARS	} by MARTINPUICH
	19		A Section reliefs carried on CORPS LINE	
			All available men were employed in improvement of shelters & the making of notched truck sections for the front line	
	21		Lt A.B. Letherman joined M.G. Coy	
	22		No 21098 Pte Taylor } wounded (Shell Shock) - 3CR to F.A.	(W Lorp Am Coy 19.11.16)
			9/Lt R.J. Grayling } taken not during the	
			2/Lt J.F. Newton	
	24		Coy relieved by 143 M.G. Coy	Casualties Killed } Pte Chinnun &c.
				No 344.94
				Wounded No 5618 Pte Burnett SgA
				SS No 9991 Pte Dalton J
				No 31851 Pte O'Halloran EJ
				No 42940 Pte Johnson J
				DR 10R. 2/Lt Martin
				C.C.F. No 1538

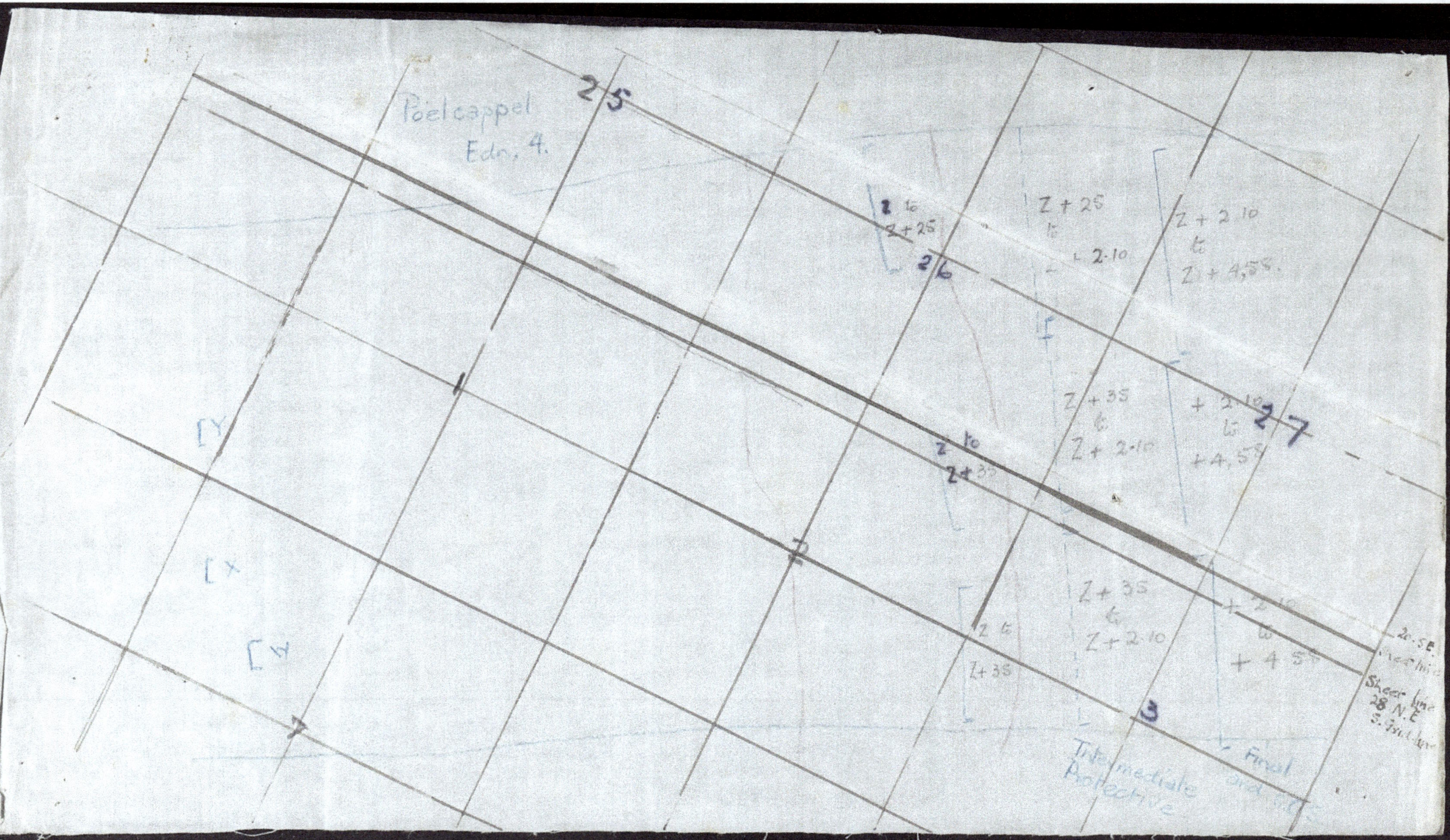

Poelcappel
Edn. 4.

25

Z+25
to
Z+2.10

Z+2.10
to

Z+35
to
Z+2.10

Z+2.10
to
Z+4.5

Z+35
to
Z+2.10

Z+2.10
to
Z+4.5

Z+35

Z to
Z+35

2·SE

Shear line
28 N.E.
S. boulder

Final

Intermediate
Protective

Shear line
28 N.E.
S. boulder

Confidential

War Diary

of

14th Machine Gun Company

from 1st November to 30th November 1916

Volume XI

www.ingramcontent.com/pod-product-compliance
Lightning Source LLC
Chambersburg PA
CBHW082010220426
43670CB00014B/2593